POSTHUMAN

BLACKNESS

and the

BLACK FEMALE

IMAGINATION

POSTHUMAN

BLACKNESS

and the

BLACK FEMALE

IMAGINATION

Kristen Lillvis

THE UNIVERSITY OF
GEORGIA PRESS

Athens

© 2017 by the University of Georgia Press
Athens, Georgia 30602
www.ugapress.org
All rights reserved
Designed by Kaelin Chappell Broaddus
Set in 9.5/14 Quadraat Regular by
Graphic Composition, Inc.

Most University of Georgia Press titles are
available from popular e-book vendors.

Printed digitally

Library of Congress Cataloging-in-Publication Data

Names: Lillvis, Kristen.
Title: Posthuman Blackness and the Black female imagination / Kristen Lillvis.
Description: Athens : The University of Georgia Press, [2017] | Includes
bibliographical references and index.
Identifiers: LCCN 2016056620| ISBN 9780820351223 (hardback : alk. paper) |
ISBN 9780820351230 (ebook)
Subjects: LCSH: American literature—African American authors—History and
criticism. | American literature—Women authors—History and criticism. |
American literature—21st century—History and criticism. | American literature—20th
century—History and criticism. | Performing arts—United States—History—21st
century. | Performing arts—United States—History—20th century. |
African Americans—Intellectual life—21st century. | African Americans—
Intellectual life—20th century. | Future, The, in literature.
Classification: LCC PS153.N5 L58 2017 | DDC 810.9/928708996073—dc23
LC record available at https://lccn.loc.gov/2016056620

CONTENTS

ACKNOWLEDGMENTS

I am grateful to the many people who made this project possible.

Thank you to the group of strong women who have served as my mentors: Giselle Liza Anatol, Kathryn Conrad, Doreen Fowler, Maryemma Graham, Susan K. Harris, and Jane Hill. Your scholarship and fellowship inspire me.

Thanks also to those individuals who read earlier incarnations of this project or otherwise provided helpful advice: Lisa Yaszek, L. Ayu Saraswati, Susan Gubar, Molly Fuller, Robert Miltner, and Amy Sherman. Thank you to the wonderful team at the University of Georgia Press, including Walter Biggins, Jordan Stepp, David E. Des Jardines, Thomas Roche, and Sue Breckenridge, for your careful attention to my manuscript.

I am grateful to my professors at Baldwin-Wallace College, Ohio University, and the University of Kansas, and to my colleagues at Marshall University, especially those in the Department of English, Honors College, and Center for Teaching and Learning. For their especially generous and important contributions, I would like to thank Johnnie Wilcox, Kelli Prejean, Anna Rollins, Laura Sonderman, Daniel O'Malley, Hilary Brewster, Jill Treftz, and Kristin Steele. I am also appreciative of the friends and colleagues I have written alongside throughout the duration of this project, including Lindsey Harper, Zelideth María Rivas, Dawn Howerton, Robert Ellison, Cody Lumpkin, Sarah A. Chavez, Walter Squire, Amy Ash, Gaywyn Moore, Alicia Sutliff-Benusis, Ali Brox, and Heather Bastian. Several other individuals have talked through this project with me; I am particularly indebted to Kent Shaw, Carrie Oeding, Allison Carey, and Eric Smith.

My ideas for this project developed during conversations at several conferences, including the Octavia Butler: Celebrating Letters, Life and Legacy Conference (2016), the Midwest Modern Language Association Conference (2016, 2015, 2014, 2012), and the American Literature Association Conference (2014). Special thanks to the students who participated in my undergraduate Honors College seminars, Technology and the Evolution of Human

Identity, and Robots, Aliens, and Black Speculative Fiction, as well as my graduate seminar, Posthuman Theory. I would especially like to acknowledge Andrew Johnston, Amber Wright, Zachery Rakes, Nathan Rucker, Steven Smith, Erica Law, and Michelle Hogmire. Extra thanks to Amber for lending her proofreading skills to the project and to Andrew for aiding me in my research on Afrofuturism.

An earlier and shorter version of chapter 1 appeared as "Becoming Self and Mother: Posthuman Liminality in Toni Morrison's *Beloved*" in *Critique: Studies in Contemporary Fiction* 54.4 (2013). Portions of my research were supported by the West Virginia Humanities Council and Marshall University's College of Liberal Arts.

This project exists because of the encouragement of family and friends: Sue Lillvis, Dean Lillvis, Joshua L. Lillvis, Katie Egging, Matt Egging, Sarah B. Hickerson, Julie Severino, Mallory Carpenter, Jessica Anderson, Craig Bantz, Lauren Kiehna, and Jana Tigchelaar. I am thankful for the care, comfort, and, when needed, distractions you provided. Thank you for everything.

Finally, I could not have begun theorizing on race, gender, and posthumanism were it not for the writers and theorists who have paved the way: Octavia E. Butler, Toni Morrison, Hortense Spillers, Sylvia Wynter, bell hooks, Peggy McIntosh, Alexander G. Weheliye, and Kodwo Eshun. I am honored to have the opportunity to highlight your work.

POSTHUMAN

BLACKNESS

and the

BLACK FEMALE

IMAGINATION

INTRODUCTION

In her mixed media collage *Do Androids Dream of How People Are Sheep?* (2010), Krista Franklin superimposes images of animals, plants, and machines onto a photograph of a black woman in profile. A tiger's torso defines the woman's forearm, while an iris encircles her upper arm. A motor fills part of her semi-transparent breast. Additional items—several raspberries, a buck's head—help to constitute the woman's skin, muscles, or bones. These magazine cutouts evoke historical and contemporary conceptions of the black woman as fighter, mother, and laborer, while other pictures, including watchband links near her heart and a vault handle at her elbow, propel the woman forward into a technophilic future. Like the cyborgs of Philip K. Dick's *Do Androids Dream of Electric Sheep?* (1968)—the science fiction novel from which the collage derives its name—the woman of Franklin's piece defies easy categorization. Both human and nonhuman, subject and object, artifact and prophet, she conveys an identity as intricate as the white lace background against which her image rests.

By blurring the boundaries of human, animal, plant, and machine in her art, Franklin points to not only the woman's complexity but also her ubiquity: she encompasses all states of existence, shaping and being shaped by what surrounds her. The Boss fashion label at the crook of her elbow, for instance, suggests the reflexive relationship between women of color and the clothing industry, a mutually constitutive association that extends from fashion houses to manufacturing plants. In the fashion world, African American designer Tracy Reese has garnered media attention for dressing First Lady Michelle Obama at the Democratic National Convention in 2012, and British designer Carly Cushnie, whose parents hail from Jamaica, and her Canadian design partner, Michelle Ochs, of German and Filipino heritage, have received acclaim for outfitting such stars as Alicia Keys, Salma Hayek, and Reese Witherspoon (Adams). Despite the success of these style makers, laborers of color face unfair and unsafe working conditions in the

United States and abroad. American retailers employ black workers in "more low paid cashier positions" and "fewer supervisory roles [. . .] relative to [their] white counterparts" (Dayen), while apparel companies have named Ethiopia "a top sourcing destination" for garment manufacturing due to "cheap labor" and "inexpensive power," a combination that in some countries—Bangladesh, for example—has led to worker exploitation and even to death (Passariello and Kapner; Jamieson, Hossain, and Bhasin). Representative of the diverse yet interconnected roles women of color occupy in the clothing industry, the Boss label affixed to the black woman in *Do Androids Dream of How People Are Sheep?* signals her liminality: her location on both sides of the dividing line between empowered and exploited, revered and reviled, honored and objectified.

In the United States, black women's liminality precedes their recognition as citizens; in fact, it predates their arrival on colonial American soil. The Middle Passage journey from Africa to the Americas placed captured Africans between continents, languages, and identities. Toni Morrison and bell hooks compare this historical reality to contemporary existence. Morrison argues that "modern life begins with slavery," since upon being enslaved, Africans experienced the "kinds of dissolution" and "madness" that characterize modern and postmodern life (qtd. in Gilroy, *Small* 178). Hooks similarly regards black women and men as representative figures in modern and postmodern societies, asserting in her essay "Postmodern Blackness"— the inspiration for my term *posthuman blackness*—that the "overall impact of postmodernism is that many other groups now share with black folks a sense of deep alienation, despair, uncertainty, loss of a sense of grounding even if it is not informed by shared circumstance" (27). According to Morrison and hooks, disorientation—a side effect of both forced and chosen border crossings—describes black life in the present as well as the past. But what about the future?

Franklin and other contemporary black artists, writers, filmmakers, musicians, and theorists record and reconfigure the black subject's experiences of liminality by blending references to the past and present with predictions for the future. Kodwo Eshun situates this blending within the cultural aesthetic of Afrofuturism. According to Eshun, Afrofuturism "reorient[s] the intercultural vectors of Black Atlantic temporality towards the proleptic as much as the retrospective," thereby pushing the black artistic "tradition of countermemory" into the future ("Further" 289). Franklin, a self-described Afrofuturist, asserts that this temporal interplay shapes her collages: "I like to pull the past and present into visual and literary spaces so they can live together," she states in an exchange with art curator Tempestt Hazel, adding during another interview, "Octavia Butler is a huge influence for me when it comes to that kind of thinking about the future and what the future looks like for us in America. For me, the future is now too: we're living in a wild time. So my view of the world is an extrapolation of the present and how we survive it" (Franklin and Hazel; Franklin and Andrews). In Afrofuturist cultural productions, historical experiences of disorientation converge with contemporary strategies for survival and futurist projections of vitality. As such, the black subject settles in multiple time periods simultaneously.

This understanding of black identity as temporally flexible, based in the history of what has occurred as well as the potential of what is to come, corresponds not only with the Afrofuturist aesthetic but also with the views of being and time found in the wider field of posthumanism, within which Afrofuturism resides. In posthuman theory, the subject—the individual, both body and mind—exists in networks of knowledge, discourse, and power that influence and are influenced by the subject. Drawing upon Gilles Deleuze and Félix Guattari's theory of "becoming," theorists such as N. Katherine Hayles, Rosi Braidotti, Judith Halberstam (who has published as J. Jack Halberstam since 2012), and Ira Livingston situate the posthuman being in a state of constant transformation that indicates the intimacy of past, present, and future temporalities as well as "self" and "other" identities. More than simply linked to the surrounding world, the posthuman subject travels "across and among" the borders of self and other, the "other" including people, communities, regimes, and technologies (Halberstam and Livingston 14). This movement indicates that the posthuman individual engages in a type of evolution that "produces nothing other than itself"— that is, the connections made between self and other within and across time are always already a part of the posthuman subject, a temporal paradox that elucidates the posthuman being's simultaneous existence in the past, present, and future (Deleuze and Guattari 238).

Consider, for example, the subjective and temporal liminality of a classic posthuman figure: the cyborg. For most people, the word *cyborg* immediately brings to mind popular man–machine amalgams, such as the Terminator, Robocop, and the Borg from *Star Trek*. With their visible blending of organic and inorganic elements—a patch of skin here, a prosthetic arm there—these cyborgs incorporate the other onto and into the self, thus breaking down and reconstituting the borderlines of identity. However, not all cyborgs display discernable inorganic or otherwise alien physical characteristics, nor, despite pop-culture imagery, do they all feature white, male flesh. Instead, cyborg boundary crossings can occur internally or even conceptually across lines of race, gender, class, sexuality, ability, and other identity factors. According to Donna J. Haraway, "fusions of outsider identities"—such as the combination of gender and racial oppressions experienced by women of color—form the "potent subjectivity" of the cyborg, which makes the cyborg "a creature of social reality as well as a creature of fiction" (174, 149).[1] Jasbir K. Puar brings Haraway's cyborg theory into conversation with intersectional feminist theory, analyzing their associations to each other and to systems of power. Puar argues that considering posthuman networks in the context of intersectional identities and, similarly, intersectional identities in the context of posthuman networks "can help us produce more roadmaps of [the] not quite fully understood relations between discipline and control" (63). She postulates that this new type of theory—itself a cyborgian joining of discrete elements—may allow those who navigate multiple marginalizations to reframe exclusionary histories, change dominant narratives, and craft more egalitarian futures (175–77).

By bringing together social theory and identity politics, posthumanism theorizes the being and bodies of individuals and their societies. I introduce the term *posthuman blackness* to describe the empowered subjectivities black women and men develop through their coincident experiences in multiple temporalities. While viewing black history and the black subject through a theory that, in its name, concerns that which is *post* human may seem parachronistic and non–subject oriented, posthuman blackness describes a temporal and subjective liminality that acknowledges the importance of history to the black subject without positing a purely historical origin for black identity. Posthumanist readings of contemporary black women's historical narratives reveal that individual agency and collective authority develop not from historical specificity but, rather, from temporal liminality.

The very term *posthumanism* expresses the boundary crossings that the theory proposes. Inquiries into the "post" in posthumanism evoke Kwame Anthony Appiah's discussion of the "post" in postmodernism and postcolonialism. Appiah argues that the prefix *post* most often functions as a "space-clearing gesture" that moves a theory (e.g. postmodernism) beyond that which preceded it (e.g. modernism) (348). However, in the case of postcolonial literature, Appiah maintains that early postcolonial texts express a shift away from colonialism and also a "return to traditions," particularly a realism that naturalizes the pre-colonial past (349). While he finds that later postcolonial literature "challenges" these "earlier legitimating narratives" (353), Appiah acknowledges the relationship between tradition and innovation in "post" theories, a temporal liminality likewise recognized by Stuart Hall. In his discussion of the "post" of post-Marxism and poststructuralism, Hall emphasizes the influence of the root theory on the theory that follows, asserting, "'[P]ost' means, for me, going on thinking on the ground of a set of established problems, a problematic. It doesn't mean deserting that terrain but rather, using it as one's reference point" (149). The complexity of "post," as outlined by Appiah and Hall, applies to the "post" of posthumanism as well: posthuman bodies—and bodies of work—cross boundaries of time, place, and culture.

Additionally, the temporal liminality of "post" theories speaks to posthumanism's indebtedness to humanism, particularly in terms of race-focused interpretations of the theories. Humanism, according to received history, centers on the liberal humanist subject, who functions as "the proprietor of his own person or capacities, owing nothing to society for them" (Macpherson 3). The liberal humanist subject's supposed "freedom from dependence on the wills of others" and unqualified possession of "his person and capacities" reveals, as feminist, postcolonial, and postmodernist theorists have pointed out, the limitations of this definition of the human for women, people of color, and the poor (Macpherson 3; Hayles 3–4; Weheliye, "'Feenin'" 23). Despite—or, rather, because of—the exclusiveness of the liberal humanist identity, many artists, writers, filmmakers, musicians, and theorists seek to discover alternative or denied notions of humanity, such as black humanism.

Black humanism rejects the supremacy of the white liberal humanist subject by considering "how humanity has been imagined and lived by those subjects excluded from this domain" (Weheliye, *Habeas* 8). In his black humanist practice, Alexander G. Weheliye turns to black women theorists such as Hortense Spillers and Sylvia Wynter, who posit "differing modes of the *human*" that emphasize "the historicity and mutability of the 'human' itself, gesturing toward different, catachrestic, conceptualizations of this category" (Wynter, "On Disenchanting" 241; Weheliye, "'Feenin'" 26). Keith Cartwright too finds that black identity and "countercultural black authority" develop out of experiences and "traumas [. . .] unaccredited in Western thinking" (11). The discovery of novel "performances of the human" in black-authored texts rectifies the historical denial of black humanity and "interrogate[s] 'other humanities'" besides the liberal humanist subject (Weheliye, "'Feenin'" 30, 40). For instance, Caroline Rody and Elizabeth Ann Beaulieu contend that black women authors, like the fictional women found within their works, return to the "mother-of-history" in an effort to reimagine "their difficult inheritance, the stories of their own genesis" (Rody 3–4; Beaulieu 25). Keith Byerman joins Rody and Beaulieu in arguing that the tales these writers tell operate in the tradition of postcolonial literatures and poststructuralist and postmodernist theories to empower diasporic peoples and "rectify the historic invisibility" of black women by "exploding the oversimplified stereotypes" offered in the dominant histories of their lives and cultures (Beaulieu 25; Rody 4–5; Byerman, *Remembering* 3, 22–23, 54). Though these scholars may not identify as practitioners of black humanism, they participate in black humanist projects by transforming the past into a present source of power for black women authors and characters, and they also highlight an opportunity for additional work on women authors' role in imagining black futures.

Posthuman theorizing, when executed with an awareness of black humanist histories, acknowledges the significance of the past to present and future ideas of black identity and simultaneously considers alternative temporal reference points for the origin of black autonomy and authority. For instance, a posthumanist reading of Beyoncé's short film *Lemonade*, released in April of 2016, emphasizes black women's liminality. References to black feminism and womanism intertwine with and develop out of visuals reminiscent of Julie Dash's film *Daughters of the Dust* (1991), poetry from Somali British poet Warsan Shire, allusions to the Yoruba water goddess Oshun, and cameos by black athletes and actors, including Serena Williams, Zendaya, Amandla Stenberg, and Quvenzhané Wallis (Roberts and Downs; Primeau). The quotes, visuals, and cameos signify the diverse cultural realms occupied by the black women featured in the film. In terms of temporality, *Lemonade* chronicles the history of black women's intersectional oppression via images of antebellum architecture, footage of the Superdome, references to infidelity, and appearances by women mourning the deaths of their unarmed black sons.[2] However, the film additionally points toward the potential of the future, with Beyoncé experiencing watery and fiery rebirths as the video

progresses through eleven stages of grief. Title overlays of the stages—
"Intuition," "Denial," "Anger," "Apathy," "Emptiness," "Accountability,"
"Reformation," "Forgiveness," "Resurrection," "Hope," and "Redemption"—
mark the linear progression of time during the film, yet they also encapsu-
late temporal liminality, representing a present-day response to a past event
("Intuition," "Denial," "Anger," "Apathy," and "Emptiness"), the restoration
of a previous peace ("Accountability" and "Forgiveness"), and the emergence
of a new state of being ("Reformation," "Resurrection," "Hope," and "Redemption"). The audio and visual references in Lemonade affirm that black
women transcend temporal and subjective boundaries, existing throughout
time and in manifold cultural, political, and personal contexts.

Given the prevalence of border crossings in black-authored art such as
Franklin's collage and Beyoncé's film, several scholars have begun investigating the relationship between posthuman liminality and black identity.
Lisa Yaszek uses Ralph Ellison's Invisible Man (1952) to point toward the
power black subjects can gain by imagining the future ("Afrofuturist"), and
Kalí Tal briefly considers notions of multiple, interconnected subjectivities
in Toni Cade Bambara's The Salt Eaters (1980). In terms of book-length literary criticism, Matthew Taylor devotes half of Universes without Us: Posthuman Cosmologies in American Literature (2013) to exploring the relationship
between race, community, and subjectivity in Charles Chesnutt's and Zora
Neale Hurston's texts. In the collection Afro-Future Females: Black Writers Chart
Science Fiction's Newest New-Wave Trajectory (2008), editor Marleen S. Barr and
her contributors examine science fiction by black women in terms of race
and gender theories, while in Afrofuturism: The World of Black Sci-Fi and Fantasy Culture (2013), Ytasha L. Womack studies black visual and performance
art, music, film, and literature through ancient and futuristic lenses. Moreover, organizers at Connecticut College, the New School, New York University, Clark Atlanta University, University of Geneva, Essex County College,
Pomona and Scripps Colleges, Loyola Marymount University, and other
higher-learning institutions have developed conferences and colloquia on
liminal spaces, places, times, and identities, all but promising that additional publications on posthumanism and race are forthcoming.[3]

Recent criticism not explicitly engaged with Afrofuturist or posthumanist theory also points toward the interconnection of distinct states of being
and time in contemporary black-authored texts. Lisa Woolfork assesses
black authors' use of the time-travel model in twentieth-century science fic-

tion and magical realism, arguing that time travel allows for lived (rather than latent) experiences of historical trauma in the present. Likewise, Ashraf H. A. Rushdy examines temporal and subjective relationships in African American fiction, situating Gayl Jones's *Corregidora* (1975), Octavia E. Butler's *Kindred* (1979), and David Bradley's *The Chaneysville Incident* (1981) as "palimpsest narratives" that consider how the history of slavery shapes contemporary people and cultures (*Remembering* 8).

Following the work of these intellectuals as well as that of Giselle Liza Anatol, Patricia Melzer, Ingrid Thaler, and Marlo David, who explore the "intersections of history and progress, tradition and innovation, technology and memory, the authentic and engineered, analog and digital" in texts by black science fiction authors and musicians (David 698), *Posthuman Blackness* asserts that the boundary crossings that exist within posthuman cultures enable black subjects to make connections to diasporic history in the present and also imagine the future as a site of power. Posthuman liminality infiltrates black visual art, film, music, and literature, including neo–slave narratives set in or focusing on the antebellum South. Neo–slave narratives, Valerie Smith argues, "illustrate the centrality of the history and the memory of slavery to our individual, racial, gender, cultural, and national identities" and "provide a perspective on a host of issues that resonate in contemporary cultural, historical, critical, and literary discourses" (168). As Smith indicates, neo–slave narratives depend on temporal liminality: stories set in the past comment on the present and create new futures.

As such, *Posthuman Blackness* asserts that contemporary black women's neo–slave narratives claim the future as fundamental to current and past conceptions of blackness. I begin by demonstrating the relevance of posthuman theory to canonical black literature—novels that have received significant and valuable readings from scholars working within the sphere of black humanism—in order to examine how historical fictions express that moving beyond the pain of the past requires an engagement with both black histories and futures. Traditional neo–slave narratives—whether published during the first wave of the genre (the 1960s to the 1980s [Misrahi-Barak 38]) or today—feature characters with a forward-looking perspective that allows them to conceive of their present and past circumstances as continually developing. Chapter 1 considers America's most famous neo–slave narrative, *Beloved* (1987), as well as Morrison's second neo–slave narrative, *A Mercy* (2008), through posthumanist theories of liminality. I argue that Morrison gestures toward a posthumanist articulation of becoming-subjectivity by positioning her women characters as simultaneously past and future oriented. Chapter 2 moves beyond an analysis of the individual and toward an examination of the community, asserting that Sherley Anne Williams's neo–slave narrative *Dessa Rose* (1986) demonstrates the shift from power structures based on difference to systems rooted in posthuman solidarity.

Chapters 3, 4, and 5 establish that posthuman theory develops and deepens the existing black humanist and Afrofuturist readings of contemporary black music, film, and science fiction. Chapter 3 serves as a bridge chapter, uniting the analysis of canonical literature from chapters 1 and 2 with an examination of popular contemporary texts. The chapter focuses on black humanist, Afrofuturist, and black posthumanist perspectives on black music, extending the existing discussions of liminal spaces, places, and bodies in Erykah Badu's and Janelle Monáe's songs and videos to Gayl Jones's blues-infused neo–slave narrative, *Corregidora*. Chapter 4 considers Middle Passage experiences in Butler's science fiction, arguing that the temporal and subjective liminality associated with the Middle Passage allows characters and readers to develop an understanding of blackness both associated with and distinct from of the ontology and cosmology of white power. Finally, chapter 5 examines two speculative texts—Sheree Renée Thomas's short story "How Sukie Cross de Big Wata" (2003) and Julie Dash's film *Daughters of the Dust* (1991)—that employ the figure of the unborn or newly born child to represent the black subject's unfixed position in time. By creating "pre-human" characters who participate in the action of historical narratives—characters who exist in history but only from a real or imagined future time following birth and maturation—Thomas and Dash promote posthuman temporal flexibility as a source of agency.

These and other examples reveal that regardless of genre, black women's historical narratives include characters that exceed the time periods into which they are written. *Posthuman Blackness* asserts that contemporary black women's texts express the potential for individual agency and collective power to develop from temporal liminality. The authors and theorists considered herein demonstrate that the boundary crossings that exist in posthuman cultures enable black subjects to make connections to diasporic histories and futures in the present. These artists, writers, musicians, and filmmakers set their stories in the past yet use their characters, particularly their women, to assert that the potential inherent in the future inspires black authority and resistance. Taken together as part of a larger collage of black culture—a collage that, in the vein of Franklin's art pieces, Beyoncé's videos, and posthumanism's liminality, develops through the assemblage of ideas, materials, and beings—these works of historical fiction depict not only the black subject's existence in the past but also her concern for and creation of that which is imminent.

CHAPTER 1

Temporal Liminality in
Toni Morrison's *Beloved* and *A Mercy*

Reading for posthuman liminality in black women's literature means that we must start simultaneously at the beginning and the end. Contemporary and even futuristic theories enhance our understanding of canonical texts, allowing us to revisit histories and ideas and interpret familiar stories in new ways. These types of border crossings pervade Toni Morrison's neo–slave narratives, *Beloved* (1987) and *A Mercy* (2008), and come to the forefront at each novel's conclusion, when the reader participates in the story's creation.

Near the close of *Beloved*, Paul D asks Sethe to consider building a future with him as she continues the work of healing from her traumatic past. "Sethe," Paul D states, "me and you, we got more yesterday than anybody. We need some kind of tomorrow" (*Beloved* 273). The bridge Paul D builds between yesterday's experiences and tomorrow's promises transforms in the final chapter of the novel into a type of mantra. Morrison compels her readers to consider the relationship of the past to the present and future through the repeated statement, "It was not a story to pass on" (*Beloved* 274–75). The reiteration of the words "to pass on" indicates both the finality of the past ("passing on" as the act of dying, of ceasing to exist in the present) and the movement of history into the future ("passing on" as the act of bequeathing knowledge or property to the next generation). As the mantra transitions from past to present tense, from "It was not a story to pass on" to "This is not a story to pass on" (*Beloved* 275), the links that connect past, present, and future become further intertwined. Despite the narrator's insistence that the story *not* be passed on, it shifts, for the reader, from relic to reality, and the narrative's continued trajectory into the future seems all but certain.

In her most recent neo–slave narrative, *A Mercy*, Morrison similarly situates her novel as an artifact that transports tales from the past into the present and future. Both Florens and her mother share stories that never make it to their intended audiences, yet these stories do not simply "talk to themselves," as Florens fears (A Mercy 188). Instead, the historical narratives gain contemporary significance due to the reader's interaction with the novel. The reader steps in to fill the role of the blacksmith, Florens's lover and the desired recipient, despite his alleged illiteracy, of the narrative she carves into the walls and floorboards of Jacob Vaark's house. Additionally, in the final chapter, the reader takes the place of Florens and hears the message that her mother "long[ed] to tell" on the day Jacob bought her daughter (A Mercy 195–96). The reader's participation in each woman's narrative ensures that the words move "beyond the eternal hemlocks"—beyond death or a forgotten history—and go on to "flavor the soil of the earth," where they will find continued life in the growth of spring (A Mercy 188).

The sense of overlapping past, present, and future temporalities that Morrison offers in Beloved and A Mercy accords with posthumanist notions of liminality. Posthuman theory provides a useful framework through which to read Morrison's neo–slave narratives and other historical narratives by black American writers, despite the seeming metachronism of studying black history through a theory that, in its name, focuses on that which is "post" human. According to posthuman theory, the subject exists within nexuses of power, knowledge, and discourse that continuously transform and are transformed by the subject. More than simply interconnected with the surrounding world, the posthuman being moves over and within the dividing lines that separate the individual from the governments, economies, technologies, communities, and people with which the individual interacts (Halberstam and Livingston 14). The problems and promise of posthuman culture stem from the multiplicity, fragmentation, and liminality of the temporalities, bodies, and subjectivities contained within—issues that, although new in terms of their relation to the posthuman subject's existence in contemporary technoculture, have been addressed by black writers and theorists for more than a century (Eshun, "Further" 301; Yaszek, "Afro-futurism" 41–60; Gilroy, Small 178). If, as Kalí Tal argues, "the struggle of African-Americans is precisely the struggle to integrate identity and multiplicity," then Morrison's Beloved and A Mercy, novels that share stories from black history and dreams of black futurity, present through their multiplicities evidence of posthuman liminality.

In *Beloved*, Morrison blurs boundaries of time and subjectivity by having Sethe, her protagonist, revisit her childhood, which allows Sethe not only to reframe and revise her traumatic history but also to position her past experiences as future focused. Although often studied as a mother, Sethe must additionally be understood as a daughter who struggles with feelings of abandonment concerning the maternal care of which she never received quite enough. Sethe's return to the position of child—a position rooted in the past yet future oriented because of the child's continuous existence in a state of becoming—opens her to possibilities, identities, and connections from which she can access and exercise greater agency.

Posthumanist understandings of temporality and subjectivity allow for a new reading of *Beloved*. In the novel, Sethe's past infiltrates her present, a temporal shift many critics have understood as immediately stifling but ultimately empowering. Elizabeth Ann Beaulieu, Missy Dehn Kubitschek, Andrea O'Reilly, and Caroline Rody find that although Sethe's history at the Sweet Home plantation plagues her present life, her "painful reacquaintance with the past," in Beaulieu's words, allows her to develop more meaningful relationships with others (and with herself) in the present (Beaulieu 71). Reading *Beloved* through posthumanism adds a new layer of complexity to the critical study of time in the novel. Sethe does not simply reimagine or rewrite her past, as many critics assert. Nor does she return to the past to lay it to rest. Instead, Sethe understands her past, like her present and future, as existing in a state of continual development. Sethe brings her past—specifically, her childhood and mother—into her present and future, and she also brings her future into the past in order to take power from the liminal subjectivity these temporal shifts engender.

The power of posthuman liminality manifests itself most clearly in Sethe's relationships with her mother and children. While critics typically conceive of the character Beloved as the return of Sethe's daughter who was killed eighteen years prior to the action in the novel's opening, Beloved's identity extends beyond this single time and this single child: she embodies the "Sixty Million and more" captive Africans who died before they reached the shores of America (Clemons 75), as well as those who survived the

Middle Passage to join the generations of the enslaved (O'Reilly 87; Horwitz 157; Bouson 152).[1] In the realm of Morrison's novel, Sethe's mother, a woman who died a violent death on the plantation where she was enslaved, must be included in this number, which means that Beloved represents not only the unnamed millions who suffered because of slavery but, for Sethe, both child and mother. Sethe therefore uses her relationship with the mysterious Beloved to resuscitate her role as a mother and her identity as a daughter. Through her return to the position of daughter, Sethe discovers a strength and forward-looking vision that allow her to begin building a future.

Because the connections between mother and child in *Beloved* transcend time and space, these lasting bonds can be considered in terms of the posthuman "becoming-subject" (Halberstam and Livingston 14). Judith Halberstam and Ira Livingston use Gilles Deleuze and Félix Guattari's theory of "becoming" to conceive of a posthuman being who experiences continual development due to a connection to surrounding elements:

> Unlike the human subject-to-be (Lacan's "l'hommelette"), who sees his own mirror image and fixed gender identity discrete and sovereign before him in a way that will forever exceed him, the posthuman becoming-subject vibrates across and among an assemblage of semi-autonomous collectivities it knows it can never either be coextensive with nor altogether separate from. The posthuman body is not driven, in the last instance, by a teleological desire for domination, death or stasis; or to become coherent and unitary; or even to explode into more disjointed multiplicities. Driven instead by the double impossibility and prerequisite to become other and to become itself, the posthuman body *intrigues* rather than desires[. . .] . (14)

Halberstam and Livingston indicate that connectivity allows the posthuman becoming-subject to exist simultaneously as self and other in the past, present, and future. Thus, posthuman theory helps articulate Sethe's dual positioning as mother and daughter as well as the potentiality of her nonlinear development. When read through posthumanism, Sethe's multiple identities take form as part of the posthuman "impossibility and prerequisite to become other and to become itself" (Halberstam and Livingston 14), which gains specificity for Sethe as the yearning to become *mother* and to become self. By developing a dual self and mother identity, Sethe incorporates her dreams for the future into her understanding of her past.

The physical and emotional bonds shared by Sethe and her children evidence the liminal identities characteristic of and the liminal temporalities inhabited by posthuman becoming-subjects. Sethe's intense connection with her children blurs the boundaries that exist between self and other, past and future. Jean Wyatt draws upon Lacan's theory of the imaginary and symbolic orders in order to argue that rather than allowing Sethe's children (or Sethe herself) to transition from the realm of imagined wholeness with the mother's body to the symbolic order of (maternal) absence and loss, Morrison creates a system that, "like Lacan's symbolic, locates subjects in relation to other subjects" but, unlike Lacan's symbolic, refuses the paternalistic mandate for physical distance between mother and child ("Giving" 475). According to Wyatt, Morrison replaces Lacan's understanding of the symbolic as a "move away from bodies touching to the compensations of abstract signifiers" with her view of a "maternal symbolic" that "makes physical contact the necessary support for Sethe's full acceptance of the separate subjectivity required by language systems" ("Giving" 484). In other words, the lasting bonds between mothers and children in Morrison's novel reveal that subjectivity depends on communal connections rather than separations. The notion of the individual developing through the community—the self forming alongside and even in conjunction with the other—corresponds with the paradox of the posthuman becoming-subject. The becoming-subject exists yet has not (and never will) fully come into being, given its impossible journey both "to become other and to become itself" (Halberstam and Livingston 14). This constant development defines posthuman subjectivity, which makes the becoming-subject an apt figure through which to study Morrison's characters.

Reading Sethe as a becoming-subject additionally requires an understanding of her dual identity as daughter and mother. Sethe not only intertwines her sense of self with the identities of her children, but her real and imagined relationships with her mother additionally shape her past, present, and future. By mothering others, Sethe attempts to bring into her present reality the physically and emotionally fulfilling mother–child relationship she never experienced during her early life because of slavery. Sethe remembers her biological mother—known to her simply as "Ma'am"—as a stranger she saw "a few times out in the fields and once when she [Ma'am] was working indigo" (Beloved 60). When telling Beloved and Denver stories of her childhood, Sethe foregrounds her physical estrangement from her mother, stating, "She didn't even sleep in the same cabin most nights I remember" (*Beloved* 60–61). Although she believes her mother must have nursed her for "two or three weeks" or at least "a week or two" during her infancy (*Beloved* 60, 203), Sethe cannot recall receiving sustenance or comfort from her biological mother. She knows only that Nan, the woman who nursed her after Ma'am returned to the fields, nursed many children and "never had enough [milk] for all" (*Beloved* 203).

The deprivation of mother's milk stands as a symbol of the maternal losses that shape Sethe's childhood and inspire her in her adult life to mother others, including Beloved. Nancy Chodorow theorizes that the physical and emotional bonds that develop between mother and child during the feeding process are as significant as the actual sustenance a child receives. Although Freud and others have argued that the bond between mother and child comes from the physiological act of breastfeeding, Chodorow adds that the physical and emotional interaction of child and mother (or child and caregiver) creates positive feelings as well (65). According to Chodorow, time spent touching the mother while receiving food not only bonds mother and child during the child's early life but also influences the child's later life as an adult.

As Chodorow's theory suggests, the absence of her mother's milk affects Sethe during her adulthood. Specifically, Sethe's early experiences with her mother shape her mothering. Sethe communicates her physical and emotional estrangement from her mother by stating that as a child she had "no nursing milk to call [her] own" (*Beloved* 200). However, as a mother, Sethe takes pride in her ability to care for her children, proclaiming that she has "milk enough for all" (*Beloved* 100).[2] When Sethe arrives at 124 Bluestone Road, her home in the free state of Ohio, her body enables her to nurse her children and also to provide for their physical and emotional comfort. Sethe celebrates the feat of surviving her escape from Sweet Home by encircling all of her children with her arms: "I was big, Paul D, and deep and wide and when I stretched out my arms all my children could get in between. I was *that* wide" (*Beloved* 162). Wyatt argues that Sethe's body takes on "mythic dimensions": her "monumental body and abundant milk give and sustain life" ("Giving" 476). The fantastical expansion Sethe envisions occurring to her body and maternal capabilities allows her to physically join with her children (they move "in between" her arms) and blur the boundaries that differentiate self and other.

Significantly, Sethe's mythic mothering shifts from giving and physically sustaining life to fulfilling her children's (especially Beloved's) emotional needs. Morrison again presents Sethe's devoted mothering in stark contrast to Ma'am's maternal absence, a juxtaposition that highlights the permeable boundaries that exist in Beloved not only between self and other but also among past, present, and future. While Ma'am lived apart from Sethe and "never fixed [her] hair nor nothing" (Beloved 60), Sethe commits herself to meeting each of Beloved's demands. Sethe feeds, clothes, and entertains Beloved by cooking and sewing with her, and she demonstrates her affection for Beloved by playing with "Beloved's hair, braiding, puffing, tying, oiling it until it made Denver nervous to watch her" (Beloved 239–40). Sethe's strategy of satisfying Beloved's physical and emotional desires by attending to her body—specifically, sating her hunger with breast milk when she is an infant and demonstrating their closeness by playing with her hair when she is a young adult—emphasizes the lasting impact of the physical and emotional relationship (or lack thereof) that exists between mother and child. In temporal terms, Sethe's negative past experiences with her mother shape her own mothering choices in the present. Ma'am's absence and Sethe's subsequent suffering inspire Sethe to protect her children from the same fate by fully—and as many critics have argued, excessively—devoting her body to her offspring.

While Sethe's maternal body provides for her children, her own daughterly body still suffers from a want of care because of her mother's absence. Sethe attempts through her mothering to heal her past and present daughterly suffering and ward off any future pain she or her children might experience. She dedicates her body to fulfilling Beloved's needs, transferring her body's power to Beloved: "The bigger Beloved got, the smaller Sethe became; the brighter Beloved's eyes, the more those eyes that used never to look away became slits of sleeplessness. Sethe no longer combed her hair or splashed her face with water. She sat in the chair licking her lips like a chastised child while Beloved ate up her life, took it, swelled up with it, grew taller on it. And the older woman yielded it up without a murmur" (Beloved 250). Sethe seeks through her mothering to strengthen her children's bodies in order to protect them—and their family link—from being appropriated by the white owner or, on a larger level, white culture.

In addition to furthering the goal of protecting her children, Sethe's tending to others and her contentment with her relational identity can be understood to develop out of her personal need for nurturance. O'Reilly argues that Sethe's mothering works to counter "the commodification of African Americans under slavery and the resulting disruption of the African American motherline," the tradition of care that unites black mothers and children (139). In positioning Sethe's mothering as a political act that empowers Sethe through the reconstitution of her motherline, O'Reilly departs from critics, including Wyatt and Demetrakopoulos, who argue that Sethe's mothering reflects her willingness to efface her individual subjectivity in favor of a relational identity (Wyatt, "Giving" 476; Demetrakopoulos 52). Venetria K. Patton and Kubitschek likewise acknowledge that Sethe's mothering is not completely self-effacing. Patton finds that "Sethe's consuming love is based on a newfound selfishness once she is in a position to claim ownership of herself and her children" (128), and Kubitschek argues that Sethe's self-interested desire to be mothered (rather than a selfish claim of ownership) motivates or contributes to her mothering of others.

Sethe seeks to assuage the pain of her past by assuming both the mother and child positions in her relationship with Beloved, which means that Beloved also exists as both mother and daughter. Morrison situates Sethe and Beloved in a mother–daughter relationship beginning the moment the childlike Beloved appears on the stump outside of 124 and Sethe feels the overwhelming urge to relieve herself, which she later understands as her water breaking (*Beloved* 51, 202). However, as their bond develops, Sethe begins to assume a daughterly role in relation to the maternal Beloved, a shift noticed by scholars including O'Reilly and Deborah Horwitz. Observing Beloved and her mother together, Denver notes, "Beloved bending over Sethe looked the mother, Sethe the teething child" (*Beloved* 250). In addition to appearance, Sethe and Beloved's behavior indicates a transformation in their relationship. Although Sethe repeatedly asserts that she believes her deceased daughter has returned in the form of Beloved, she relates to Beloved as if the young woman were a reincarnation of her mother, not her daughter. Sethe compares her relationship with Beloved to her relationship with her mother, stating that Beloved "came right on back like a good girl, like a daughter which is what I wanted to be and would have been if my ma'am had been able to get out of the rice long enough before they hanged her and let me be one" (*Beloved* 203). While Sethe initially views Beloved's actions as a daughter's departure from and subsequent return to her mother, as she continues to consider their situation, she focuses on maternal (rather than daughterly) absences: "I wonder what they [her mother and the other women] was doing when they was caught. Running, you think? No. Not that. Because she was my ma'am and nobody's ma'am would run off and leave her daughter, would she?" (Beloved 203). Sethe's turn toward memories of her mother's absence indicates that Beloved becomes a stand-in not for the devoted daughter who returns to the mother but the good mother who refuses to abandon (and, hence, returns to) her daughter.

The interior monologues Morrison presents in part 2 of her novel support a reading of Beloved as Sethe's mother and reinforce the existence of circular or liminal temporalities in Beloved. In Beloved's monologue, readers bear witness to the movement of the past into the present and future (and vice versa) through Beloved's descriptions of the mother's return to the daughter and the daughter's return to the mother during the Middle Passage. Morrison first introduces Sethe's mother's Middle Passage experience through Nan, who tells a young Sethe that "her mother and Nan were together from the sea" (Beloved 62). In her interior monologue, Beloved reveals additional details about the Middle Passage, particularly as it relates to the mother–daughter experience during slavery. Like Sethe, who throughout Morrison's novel returns again and again to her memory of her lost mother, Beloved centers her monologue on a particular figure: the woman with "the face that is mine" (Beloved 211). Beloved describes the woman multiple times, focusing on her desire to be seen by the woman and her need to "join" with her in some way (Beloved 213): "I am not separate from her   there is no place where I stop   her face is my own and I want to be there in the place where her face is and to be looking at it too" (Beloved 210). Beloved's insistence on her bodily connection to the woman as well as the very nature of her expression—her narrative is almost wholly absent of punctuation that would mark the end of one idea and the beginning of the next—indicate that the woman Beloved references is her mother, and the two exist in the realm of intense mother–child connection known as the imaginary or semiotic chora. Reading Beloved's monologue through Julia Kristeva's theory of the child's pre-oedipal union with the mother, Claudine Raynaud argues that Beloved's narrative "hints at a desire for fusion, for a world where mother and daughter can be together, reunited in an embrace that reproduces the oneness of pregnancy" (76). As Raynaud's assessment of the Middle Passage scene indicates, Beloved joins Sethe in seeking the comfort of the mother–child connection, and this yearning only intensifies when the woman, her mother, "goes in the water" (presumably, she commits suicide), taking their shared face with her (*Beloved* 212).

The loss of her mother results for Beloved in the loss of her own identity—that is, until the mother returns. If Sethe mothers others in order to make up for the maternal absences she suffered as a child, this pattern of behavior can be understood to begin with her own mother. In her interior monologue, Beloved indicates that she reconnects to her mother by giving birth to Sethe, through whom she can once again "see her face which is mine" (*Beloved* 212). Upon Sethe's birth, which Beloved understands as the rebirth of her own mother, Beloved revises history by giving a name to the woman on the ship; she states definitively, "Sethe went into the sea. She went there" (*Beloved* 214). Beloved expresses her maternal devotion to her daughter Sethe as well as her daughterly desire for the mother's return: "the sun closes my eyes   when I open them I see the face I lost   Sethe's is the face that left me   Sethe sees me see her and I see the smile   her smiling face is the place for me   it is the face I lost   she is my face smiling at me   doing it at last" (*Beloved* 213). Just as Sethe mothers Beloved in the present in the hopes of reconnecting to her own mother in the future, Beloved mothers Sethe in an effort to finally "join" with the mother she lost during the Middle Passage, to both *see* and *be* the face she was so fond of in the past.

By mothering in order to make up for the daughterly deprivations they suffered in their youths, Beloved and Sethe participate, traditionally and nontraditionally, in the reproduction of mothering. According to Chodorow, social systems in which the mother is the primary parent produce female children who as adults desire to mother as a means of recreating a "relational triangle": "As a result of being parented by a woman and growing up heterosexual, women have different and more complex relational needs in which an exclusive relationship with a man is not enough. [. . .] [T]his is because women situate themselves psychologically as part of a relational triangle in which their father and men are emotionally secondary or, at most, equal to their mother and women" (199). Chodorow asserts that because of her relational identity, a woman cannot be emotionally fulfilled through a relationship with a man, but she can have her emotional needs met by having a child (200–01). Becoming a mother completes a woman's triangular relational needs because the woman relates to her child as both a mother and a daughter (Chodorow 204). A woman with a child identifies with her mother, feeling a sense of responsibility to her child as well as a desire to either recreate positive pre-oedipal experiences or "get back at her mother for (fantasied) injuries done by her mother to her" (Chodorow 204, 90). Additionally, this woman experiences an "empathetic identification" with her child—that is, she sees herself in or as her child—due to her "unconscious investment in reactivating" her pre-oedipal relationship with her mother (Chodorow 204).

Beloved and other texts in which mother–child bonds are broken at a young age cannot easily be read according to Chodorow's theory of the relational triangle, which assumes the mother's presence in her child's early life.[3] O'Reilly asks, "If the ability to mother is developmentally built into the daughter's personality through the mother–daughter bond—she acquires a relational self, which in turn becomes a maternal self—what happens when that crucial bond is denied, damaged, or destroyed as it was in slavery?" (88). In Morrison's novel, slavery disrupts Sethe's relationship with her mother and prevents her from forming affective bonds with her other caretakers. However, Sethe can still be understood to perceive the mother–child relationship as one in which mother and child are united—as one through which she can become self and other. Psychoanalytic theorist Jessica Benjamin asserts that the "vision of perfect oneness" associated with the early mother–child relationship "is an ideal—a symbolic expression of our longing—that we project onto the past" (173). Unlike Chodorow, who fails to consider "the sociohistorical displacement of the mother–child relationship" in her theory of relational identification (O'Reilly 88), Benjamin argues that broken mother–child bonds facilitate the child's fantasy of connection to the mother: "This ideal [of mother–child unity] becomes enlarged in reaction to the experience of helplessness—in the face of circumstance, powerlessness, death—but also by the distance from mother's help that repudiation of her [following the oedipal crisis] enforces" (173). Benjamin states that the imagined connection between mother and child ensures the child "the possibility of regaining"—or, as Morrison's novel demonstrates, gaining for the first time—"the satisfactions of dependency," including the confidence that the child's needs can and will be fulfilled (174).

The convergence of past, present, and future in Benjamin's theory of mother–child unity corresponds with an understanding of the posthuman becoming-subject's existence within a liminal temporality. In addition to looking at the intersection of multiple time periods, posthuman theory explicates how the child might perceive a connection between self and mother despite the absence of evidence. While in their theorizing of the posthuman subject Halberstam and Livingston reject psychoanalytic metaphors of mother–child connection and triangular family structures, they assert that the posthuman being is necessarily linked to the surrounding world: "The dependence or interdependence of bodies on the material and discursive networks through which they operate means that the umbilical cords that supply us (without which we would die) are always multiple" (17). Rather than questioning the subject's reliance on surrounding networks and beings, we must, Halberstam and Livingston argue, refuse to "distinguish absolutely or categorically between bodies and their material extensions" (17). Moved by the desire both "to become other and to become itself," the posthuman being must be understood to embody multiple links to others.

Reading *Beloved* through the lens of posthumanism reveals that Sethe participates in the reproduction of mothering not because of a relational identity established during her infancy (as outlined by Chodorow) but rather because of the fantasy of mother–child unity—the expression of her desire to become self and other—that develops during her childhood, adolescence, and adult life. O'Reilly similarly argues that "the daughter's eventual maternal subjectivity is determined less by the way she was mothered and more by how she perceived her own mother" (89). However, rather than asserting that the reproduction of mothering makes Sethe's becoming-subjectivity possible, O'Reilly, like Barbara Schapiro, finds that Sethe learns from her mother not to understand herself as an independent subject (O'Reilly 90; Schapiro 197).

While Sethe's perceived connection with her mother extends beyond her childhood, the bond functions as a past-, present-, and future-based source of power that allows Sethe to develop as a subject. Sethe believes that she has a profound connection to her biological mother, even if she did not recognize this connection during her early years. As Sethe makes her escape from Sweet Home, the movement of her child in her womb evokes her memory of men and women (including her Ma'am) on the plantation where she was born dancing "the antelope": "They shifted shapes and became something other. Some unchained, demanding other whose feet knew her pulse better than she did. Just like the one in her stomach" (*Beloved* 31). Sethe associates the movements of the child in her womb (a symbol of her future) with her mother's dancing (a memory of her past). Creating this liminal temporality allows her to see the family as united and mothering as a means by which she communes with her daughter as well as her mother.

Morrison further portrays liminal notions of temporality and subjectivity through Sethe's imaginings of her mother's unique love for her, a love Ma'am refused to share with the children who, unlike Sethe, were born out of the many sexual assaults she suffered (*Beloved* 62, 201). Although Sethe never had the opportunity to match her mother's love with her own, she believes that she would have been a devoted daughter: "I would have tended my own mother if she needed me. If they had let her out of the rice field, because I was the one she didn't throw away. I couldn't have done more for [Mrs. Garner] than I would my own ma'am if she was to take sick and need me and I'd have stayed with her till she got well or died. And I would have stayed after that except Nan snatched me back" (*Beloved* 200–01). While Sethe associates her relationship with Nan, the community caregiver, as one rooted in the past—Sethe perceives Nan as snatching her "back," taking her from a future-oriented position where she has the potential to develop a relationship with her mother to the position of loss she has experienced in the past—she views her connection with her mother as one that persists beyond death: she states that her plan to protect her children and herself from schoolteacher "was to take [them] all to the other side where [her] own ma'am is" (*Beloved* 203). Not only was she willing as a child to tend to her mother's dead body, but as an adult Sethe desires to unite her mother and her children in the afterlife.

While scholars have investigated how the women of *Beloved* draw upon their experiences as "loved daughter[s]" in order to gain access to "empowering female models" (Kubitschek 172), these scholars typically situate the power Morrison's mothers provide as historical. Kubitschek argues, for example, that the black women Morrison features in her novel draw upon "historical strength imaged as a mother" (177). According to Rody, this understanding of the mother–child bond as one through which women access historical power extends across the larger body of black women's texts: "In the heroines of this literature, female desire stages a rendezvous with the hazard of history itself, daring to be overcome with history, to experience the self as the juncture of historical forces, to realize daughterhood in a kind of historical sublime" (16). While the focus on the past promoted in much of the existing scholarship concerning black women authors and their texts productively recovers previously unwritten histories of diasporic families and communities, understanding the mother–child bond as past, present, and future oriented allows diasporic daughters such as Sethe to connect not only to empowering histories but also energizing new futures from which they can gain personal and political power. Sethe's past—namely, her connection to an historical and cultural motherline—may give her strength to reimagine her life and, as Kubitschek argues, emerge from the horrors she suffered (170). Yet this past, much like Sethe's present and projected future, must be understood as mutable and, more importantly, contingent upon Sethe's current and coming experiences. As a becoming-subject, Sethe lives within a nonlinear temporality, where her future changes her past in the same way her past shapes her future.

Certainly, reading Sethe's state of daughterly development, her becoming-subjectivity, as advantageous can be difficult, considering the bodily toll this type of existence takes: Sethe nearly loses herself to Beloved's destructive mothering. Lisa Yaszek points out that building a posthuman identity—in this case, embracing the liminality of past, present, and future temporalities and self and other subjectivities—always involves loss. She asserts that "subjects cannot expect to decolonize themselves and construct new forms of agency without widespread and sometimes unexpectedly painful results" (Yaszek, Self 93). In Beloved Sethe's return to the position of daughter causes her to experience the pain Yaszek references, but Sethe also finds power in her new identity. Sethe's rebirth—her existence as someone free from the confines of a repeating past in which she has no agency—allows her to blossom in ways she could not before. Specifically, her return to a childlike state enables her to see the world (and her own history) in a new light, both literally and figuratively. Before Beloved returned and Sethe reproduced herself as a child, Sethe found herself paralyzed by her past: "her brain was not interested in the future. Loaded with the past and hungry for more, it left her no room to imagine, let alone plan for, the next day" (Beloved 70). Yet once Sethe perceives the return of her mother in the form of Beloved, she grants herself permission to relive her childhood and experience a relationship with her mother. As she goes through this rebirth, Sethe imagines signs of regeneration in the world that surrounds her:

> Now I can look at things again because she's here to see them too. After the shed, I stopped. Now, in the morning, when I light the fire I mean to look out the window to see what the sun is doing to the day. Does it hit the

pump handle first or the spigot? See if the grass is gray-green or brown or what. [. . .] Think what spring will be for us! I'll plant carrots just so she see them, and turnips. Have you ever seen one, baby? A prettier thing God never made. White and purple with a tender tail and a hard head. Feels good when you hold it in your hand and smells like the creek when it floods, bitter but happy. We'll smell them together, Beloved. Beloved. (Beloved 201)

Sethe rewrites her history by imagining a future with her daughter/mother. The pleasure Sethe takes in the present from remembering experiences she had in the past (such as the pleasant smell of a turnip) and projecting the experiences she and Beloved will share in the coming spring reveals how temporality shifts when Sethe feels empowered (or, alternatively, how Sethe gains power from temporal shifts). Sethe's desire to shape her life reconfigures her existence as an embodied subject: both she and Beloved exist in the past, present, and future as daughter and mother.

Although Sethe embraces her daughterly role and enjoys the possibility her future holds, Beloved's mothering becomes threatening to her. Accordingly, the other mother figures who surround Sethe must help her navigate her new childhood and create (and take power in) a better past, present, and future. Denver, who early in the novel joins Sethe in participating in the reproduction of mothering by caring for Beloved, continues her maternal role in her relation to Sethe. Denver's decision to become a mother can be understood as a strategy for having her own needs fulfilled. Like Sethe, Denver participates in the reproduction of mothering in an attempt to reconnect to her mother, who has become consumed by her care for Beloved. While at times Denver seems to reject Sethe to focus on Beloved, Denver's actions can still be understood as a reproduction of mothering: she strives to become deeply connected to Beloved in order to have her own daughterly needs met. When Denver discovers that her mothering of Beloved does not satisfy her needs, she transitions to giving her maternal care directly to her own mother. Denver provides for her mother by working outside of the home and returning to 124 with food. She also reunites her mother with a community of women who can help fulfill Sethe's need for nurturance.

With the aid of Denver and the women her daughter calls to action, Sethe gains the opportunity to reenact a specific moment from her past—schoolteacher's arrival at 124—and reconcile that experience with her new understanding of herself as both a daughter and a mother. When Sethe mistakes Edward Bodwin (who arrives at 124 to bring Denver to work) for schoolteacher, she feels the fear and rage she felt when schoolteacher arrived eighteen years earlier. However, Sethe changes her behavior. Rather than repeating her past actions and turning the ice pick in her hand against Beloved, Sethe runs at Bodwin/schoolteacher. While the change in Sethe's action is significant—it shows that Sethe has embraced her movement toward the future and can imagine different outcomes to schoolteacher's arrival, thus attempting to recreate the past—even more important is the community's reaction to Sethe. Denver and the women outside of the house on Bluestone Road act as protective mothers to Sethe, giving her the care she desired from her biological mother and which she provides for her children. Although Sethe does not willingly refrain from attacking Bodwin, the community forces her to submit to their mothering: they stop her from killing by physically directing her focus away from her history (as personified by Bodwin/schoolteacher) and toward the present group of mothers gathered in her yard. Accordingly, Beloved—the mother of Sethe's past—disappears, and Sethe finds herself surrounded by multiple "othermothers" who can continue ushering her into a new future (Collins 51).

Morrison further shows Sethe's shift from being preoccupied by an unchanging past to showing concern for the coming future through her depiction of Sethe's relationship with Paul D. Paul D joins Denver and the women who protect Sethe outside of 124 in acting as a mother to the childlike Sethe. He facilitates her development by attending to her bodily needs (offering to rub her feet) and emotional health (encouraging her to continue living after Beloved's disappearance) (Morrison, Beloved 271–72; Wyatt, "Giving" 484). As Wyatt argues, Paul D occupies the "restorative maternal role"—the role of physical and spiritual healer—"once occupied by Baby Suggs" ("Giving" 484). Paul D does not simply fulfill Sethe's needs, but, like Baby Suggs, he shows Sethe how to exercise her own subjectivity so that she can develop personal strength. With Paul D's help, particularly his insistence that Sethe's life is valuable and she is her own "best thing" (Beloved 273), Sethe begins the process of recovering from her oppressive history.

Moreover, Paul D aids Sethe in continuing her nonlinear development by urging her not only to rebuild her past but also to simultaneously construct a future. Like Baby Suggs—whose name emphasizes the mother's role as a daughter or "Baby" (Rody 92)—Paul D confounds linear views of identity and time. He asserts that he and Sethe "got more yesterday than any-body" and "need some kind of tomorrow," which conveys that the direction of Sethe's new life need not be determined by her earlier existence (*Beloved* 273). Through the return to the position of child, Sethe connects to her past but moves forward, taking power in the potentiality of her future.

A posthumanist reading of the bonds that join mother and child in Morri-son's *Beloved* offers a new way of understanding the past, present, and future in black women's literature: as linked temporalities through which agency can be accessed and empowered identities and communities can be created. *Beloved* ends, fittingly, with Sethe in a state of becoming: she has just begun to recognize herself as a person with value. The various readings available for her final spoken words, "Me? Me?", speak to the possibility inherent in her new attitude. The repetition of "me," significantly stated two times, can be understood to reference Sethe's liminal or multiple identity: she is both daughter and mother, self and other. By forging these links across time and personhood, Sethe begins the work of healing from her past pains and cre-ating a better present and future life.

PAST, PRESENT, AND FUTURE
IDENTITIES IN A MERCY

In *A Mercy*, just as in *Beloved*, characters transcend the boundaries of time and subjectivity. In *Beloved* Morrison expresses liminality through Sethe's return to her childhood, a return that enables Sethe to review her past pains and reconsider them in the context of an imagined future. While tempo-ralities similarly commingle in *A Mercy*, Florens's history initially appears to overwhelm rather than overlap her present experiences and future plans. Florens tells of her childhood separation from her mother, but she does not limit her mother to her past; instead, Florens projects her historical relation-ship with her mother into the present and future, reconstituting her role as scorned daughter in her memories of her mother, her interactions with Widow Ealing and Daughter Jane, and her connection to the blacksmith. Al-though Florens states that she desires to revise her childhood experience of rejection, she initially relives the rejection, which impedes her development of a relational and liminal subjectivity.

While *A Mercy*, even more so than *Beloved*, reveals the difficulty of em-bracing the future for those who have suffered broken bonds during slavery,

Morrison's ninth novel follows *Beloved* in reflecting posthuman conceptions of temporal and subjective liminality. Florens struggles throughout the narrative with the weight of her history, but she ultimately projects herself forward into an uncertain—but potentially more empowering—future. The overwhelming presence of history in the novel makes especially important the search for those places where Florens imagines coming events. By positioning herself as a subject who belongs not only to the past but also the present and future, Florens shows that a liminal view of temporality can extend to a liminal and, ultimately, relational, understanding of identity. Rather than existing as "a thing apart" (*A Mercy* 135), Florens moves throughout space and time along networks that join her even to those individuals, including her absent mother, by whom she once found herself rejected.

Reading Florens as the possessor of a relational identity proves difficult, considering that she constructs the narrative of her life as one defined by separation. Florens's mother offers her daughter to Jacob Vaark, a Dutch trader and farmer, in the hopes that the girl will escape the sexual abuse that plagues the women enslaved by D'Ortega in Maryland. Only eight years old, Florens perceives her mother's mercy as a rejection. According to Naomi Morgenstern, "There are profound echoes of *Beloved*" in the scenes of maternal separation featured in *A Mercy*, and like in *Beloved*, the broken bonds in *A Mercy* shape the subjectivity of Morrison's characters: "it is not only that Florens tries to read a message"—her mother's motivation for dismissing her—"from which she is cut off (both on the level of the realist plot and on the level of the narrative structure) but also that this message constitutes her as a subject" (16). Like Sethe, Florens believes herself to be abandoned by her mother, and this historical desertion shapes her present and future interactions with others.

Because her separation from her mother shapes her identity, Florens relives the past event again and again. Time, for Florens, does not operate linearly; instead, temporalities—and those who inhabit them—overlap and intersect. Florens tells others that her mother has died, yet she resurrects her mother throughout the narrative, questioning whether the woman and her son, Florens's brother, will "ever decide to rest" and positing that the two live "many lives beyond" death and visit in the form of owls, dream figures, and ghosts (*A Mercy* 7, 127, 161–63). Since Florens's mother materializes during the narrative's present-situated events, Florens understands this figure and her history with her as continuous, part of an ongoing drama rather than relegated to the past.

As Florens carries her identity as daughter out of her history and into her present and future, she blurs the boundaries between her eight-year-old self (her age when separated from her mother) and her sixteen-year-old self (her age during the novel's present setting). In blending these two versions of her identity, Florens demonstrates the characteristics of a posthuman becoming-subject motivated "by the double impossibility and prerequisite to become other and to become itself" (Halberstam and Livingston 14). While in *Beloved* Sethe manifests this liminality in her desire to become *mother* and to become self, in *A Mercy* Florens exhibits posthuman liminality—subjective and temporal—in her longing to become *daughter* and to become self: to bring into the present her desired future position as another's daughter and also to bring into the present her past existence as her mother's daughter.

By uniting these aspects of her personality, Florens expresses a liminal and, ultimately, relational identity that joins her, regardless of distance and time, to multiple mothers: she adopts the new position as daughter to several other mother figures in order to form a more fulfilling relational bond, and she also attempts to resuscitate her identity as daughter and reconstitute her original relationship with her mother. Considering the first aspect of this liminal identity—the wish to make real in the present her imagined future position as another's daughter—Florens finds a surrogate mother in Lina, a Native American woman and slave on Vaark's farm who gives Florens clothing, shelter, and love.[4] Despite the differences in her perceptions of her birthmother and Lina, Florens obfuscates the borderlines that separate the women, shifting, for example, from the recollection of her mother criticizing her taste for high heels to the memory of Lina securing her boots (*A Mercy* 4). As Florens associates her birthmother and Lina, she makes connections between two versions of herself as daughter, one rejected and the other loved.

Florens acquires several additional mother figures in her search to become another's daughter and fulfill the posthuman imperative to join the identity of other (loved child) with the identity of self (rejected child). During the early part of her stay with Widow Ealing and Daughter Jane, Florens exhibits a relational identity. Florens may not find the attentive mother she desires in Widow Ealing, considering that the Widow expresses suspicion regarding Florens's dark skin and sudden appearance, but Widow Ealing and Jane do take on maternal roles relative to Florens's daughterly position. Florens finds herself brought into the family as she, rather than the biological daughter, Jane, shares a meal with Widow Ealing. Additionally, Florens looks to Jane for guidance on how to behave in the widow's presence (*A Mercy* 129–30). Florens links her role with the Ealings to her other networks of connection, including the community on Vaark's farm (she carries a letter that certifies her belonging to the Vaarks) and her birth family in Maryland. Ensconced in networks that transcend spatial and temporal restrictions, Florens initially appears to be a posthuman subject who embraces a relational identity, though making links across space and time reminds her in the present of losses from her past.

Recollections of her painful history as well as repeated maternal dismissals in the present thwart Florens's efforts to supplement in a sustainable way her historical role as denied daughter with any other identity. Accordingly, when taking shelter with Widow Ealing and Daughter Jane, Florens shifts from a multiple or liminal self—as evidenced by her blurring of subjective and temporal borderlines—to a purely historical personality. When a group of religious zealots arrives at Widow Ealing's home, Florens relives the rejection she experienced at the moment of sale. Florens encounters among the villagers "a little girl" who, she states, "reminds me of myself when my mother sends me away" (*A Mercy* 130). Although Florens identifies with the child and, in doing so, situates herself as a member—a daughter—of the village, the child and accompanying adults reject her: "I am thinking how sweet she [the little girl] seems when she screams and hides behind the skirts of one of the women. Then each visitor turns to look at me. The women gasp. The man's walking stick clatters to the floor causing the remaining hen to squawk and flutter. He retrieves his stick, points it at me saying who be this? One of the women covers her eyes saying God help us. The little girl wails and rocks back and forth" (*A Mercy* 130–31). Viewed by the white villagers as the devil's "minion" because of her dark skin, Florens shifts her identity from a member of multiple communities to "a thing apart" (*A Mercy* 131, 135). Specifically, she loses her imagined association with the villagers, her potential friendship with Daughter Jane, and the physical record of connection (the letter) that links her to the Vaark farm when she flees the Ealings' house. Florens's three-part return to the position of rejected child dissolves her relational identity; truly, she becomes "a thing apart."

As a result of losing her relational identity, Florens temporarily abandons her engagement with the present and future—two of the multiple temporalities to which she was previously linked—and assumes a purely historical position. She states that she sees herself as "a weak calf abandon by the herd, a turtle without shell, a minion with no telltale signs but a darkness [she is] born with" (A Mercy 135), characteristics she associates more with her past abandonment than her present dismissal. According to Wyatt, throughout A Mercy Florens views her present through the lens of the past, including during her interaction with the villagers: "For Florens, the message is again rejection; although on this second occasion it is a repudiation of her black body by strangers, the intensity of the experience is heightened by its repetition of the original maternal rejection" ("Failed" 135). While Florens enters the Ealing household with a liminal and relational identity, she feels overcome by her history after experiencing the villagers' repudiation.

The most profound example of a repeated maternal rejection and the resulting severing of a relational identity occurs during Florens's time at the blacksmith's home. Following her stay with Widow Ealing and Daughter Jane, Florens commits herself to reconstituting her original mother–daughter relationship, and she abandons the posthumanist project of becoming another's daughter as well. Although Florens takes the blacksmith as her lover, he also occupies the mother position in Florens's resurrected relational triangle. Wyatt argues that Florens locates herself "within the maternal matrix of the blacksmith's love," given that her bond with the blacksmith exhibits "a symbiotic form reminiscent of a young child's dependency on the mother" ("Failed" 136). Morgenstern likewise asserts that the blacksmith functions as "a substitute for that original maternal object" and reveals Florens's preoccupation with the past, given that "the present-tense narrative of Florens's journey to find the blacksmith performs a displacement and repetition of a return to the mother" (15). With the blacksmith standing in for her absent mother, Florens resumes her daughterly position from the past in an attempt to achieve emotional contentment.

The temporal liminality in Florens's narrative of and to the blacksmith reveals that she, like Sethe, can revise her traumatic history by imagining a more fulfilling future. However, rather than reconfiguring the past—viewing her history from a present- or even future-oriented position—Florens revivifies it. While Sethe's vision for the future allows her to recreate her childhood and experience a relationship with her mother, Florens's preoccupation with the past intrudes into her present life with the blacksmith. When considering their time together, Florens states, "I don't say what I am thinking. That I will stay. That when you return from healing Mistress whether she is live or no I am here with you always. Never never without you. Here I am not the one to throw out. No one steals my warmth and shoes because I am small. No one handles my backside. No one whinnies like sheep or goat because I drop in fear and weakness. No one screams at the sight of me. No one watches my body for how it is unseemly. With you my body is pleasure is safe is belonging" (A Mercy 161). Florens begins with an assertion of future plans ("I will stay"), but she moves quickly into memories of past events stated in the present tense ("With you my body is pleasure is safe is belonging"). Her use of present tense reveals that, as Wyatt argues, Florens's past "merges with the present," causing her to experience her history "absolutely in her present" life ("Failed" 135, 138). Moreover, Florens's use of negative constructions—for example, rather than saying, "Here I am chosen and loved," she asserts, "Here I am not the one to throw out"—indicates that her present relationship has relevance because it stands in opposition to her mother's past rejection. If Florens understands her current life in terms of the perceived dismissal from her past, then her present falls under the purview of this history.

In addition to pervading her present, Florens's past infiltrates her future with her lover. Florens makes reference to the future when discussing her bond with the blacksmith, but she gives her past priority, imagining her future as either a revision or, more likely, reproduction of her history. After seeing that the blacksmith has taken a small boy, Malaik, into his care, Florens projects her fear of rejection—a product of her broken bond with her mother—into the future, stating, "I worry as the boy steps closer to you. How you offer and he owns your forefinger. As if he is your future. Not me" (A Mercy 160). In the presence of the boy, Florens's thoughts about subsequent times interweave with her perception of the past, and she dreams that Malaik takes the place of her baby brother, holding not the blacksmith's finger but her mother's hand (A Mercy 162). Although she desires change and, specifically, a loving parent–child relationship for herself, Florens reveals through this dream that she views her future as under the assault of historical forces, and she "feel[s] the clutch inside" (A Mercy 162), a physical response to the rejection that she expects will plague her again.

According to Florens's perception of Malaik, the boy fulfills the posthuman "double impossibility and prerequisite to become other and to become itself" (Halberstam and Livingston 14); specifically, he embodies brother and self. The liminality in Florens's vision of Malaik indicates a potential opportunity for Florens to not revive but revise her understanding of her past—to consider her perspective as well as her brother's and mother's—but, instead, Florens allows her history to consume her. Although she declares, "This expel can never happen again," which shows that she envisions a more positive future and sees her negative past experiences as malleable or at least not dictatorial, Florens preserves her position as "a thing apart" (A Mercy 162, 135). Faced with the threat of rejection, she chooses, first, to "hide [her] head" under the blacksmith's blanket and, later, pull Malaik's arm and attack the blacksmith with a hammer and tongs (A Mercy 163–67, 184–85). By either ignoring or attacking those who would cast her out, Florens remains outside the relational triangle in a position of difference first suggested by her mother (as Florens continues to perceive her) and later confirmed by Widow Ealing's visitors as well as Malaik and the blacksmith. Rather than embracing a relational and, ultimately, liminal identity, Florens finds herself rooted in space and time as the rejected daughter, a figure that developed from a particular moment in her childhood.

The institution of slavery—which breaks mother–child bonds—bears responsibility for Florens's inability to move beyond her historical experience of separation and to sustain a relational identity. As Maxine L. Montgomery acknowledges, Morrison asserts that the "anxiety of belonging" inscribed in "the central metaphors" of national and international discourses on power systems develop out of racial constructs (Morrison, "Home" 10; Montgomery 628). Morrison highlights the ongoing presence of racial oppression in these and other discourses through Florens's historically situated and relationally separated subjectivity. According to Wyatt, "Florens cannot have a retroactive understanding of the mother's seeming rejection because, irrevocably separated by sale, she cannot receive her mother's explanatory message" ("Failed" 138). Nor can Florens revise her role in the relationship by gaining a new perspective due to her age and maturity, Wyatt asserts, since "her development was arrested at the time her mother cast her aside," or, again, the moment of sale ("Failed" 138).

Florens's stunted emotional growth explains why even in the liminal space of Vaark's farm, a space occupied by figures who, Montgomery argues, "form a potentially unlimited set of communal configurations" (631),

Florens cannot maintain a relational identity. The novel asserts that those on the Vaark farm "were not a family—not even a like-minded group. They were orphans, each and all" (A Mercy 69). However, Mina Karavanta states, the inhabitants operate as part of a network, "community," or "commons shared by heterogeneous others and their risky acts of care and mercy" (736). The blurring of these "heterogeneous" individuals into a common network reveals their liminal movement between self and other identities. However, while Florens joins Lina, Sorrow, Will, Scully, Rebekka, and Vaark in their mutual pursuits, she positions herself outside of their network of connection, identifying instead as "bad," "wild," and "wilderness" (A Mercy 4, 189). Moreover, Florens fails to form a liminal identity in her relationship with the blacksmith, but rather than seeing herself as independent from her lover, she positions him as her "shaper," "world," and "own[er]" (A Mercy 83, 166). Florens's separation from her mother and the experiences of rejection that follow foster in her either an independent or reliant personality rather than a relational identity.

While slavery's perversion of family relationships causes Florens to re-ject community in favor of disconnection or dependency, the past does not determine black power (or the lack thereof) in the novel. A posthumanist reading of A Mercy reveals that despite her preoccupation with the past, Flo-rens ultimately claims the temporal liminality—including a concern for the future—indicative of a becoming-subject. Florens brings her past into the present throughout her narrative to the blacksmith, but the conclusion of the novel indicates that she embraces the interplay of past, present, and future temporalities.

After being rejected by the blacksmith, Florens reassesses her under-standing of her history. Her history is no longer stagnant: her views of the present shape the way she sees the past. Florens speaks in the present tense of her former feelings about the blacksmith—including what she once as-sumed would be her future relationship with her lover—when she states, "[M]y way is clear after losing you who I am thinking always as my life and my security from harm, from any who look closely at me only to throw me away" (A Mercy 184). She gives her history continued life by writing of her past feelings in the present tense, but her assessment of her history has changed: her statements now point to the invalidity of her past feelings. While her his-tory shapes her existence in other temporalities—her "way," or her path for the future, "is clear" based on the events that have occurred—this history does not rule her. Indeed, Florens acknowledges that her thoughts in the present shape the way she views her history. She asserts that her past beliefs shift from certainties to inaccuracies when viewed in the context of her present: "In the beginning when I come to this room I am certain the telling will give me the tears I never have. I am wrong" (A Mercy 185). Florens's history may move into other temporalities, but because she acknowledges that her assertion of her history's concreteness was incorrect, Florens presents both time and subjectivity as changeable.

By the end of A Mercy, Florens transitions from a fixation with the past to a broader engagement with multiple temporalities. The final three paragraphs of her narration contain eight occurrences of the auxiliary verb will, and these statements of what the future will hold mix with assertions about her past experiences and present actions. For example, when considering the coming days, Florens states, "I am near the door and at the closing now. What will I do with my nights when the telling stops? Dreaming will not come again. Sudden I am remembering" (A Mercy 188). Present-tense declarations transition into concerns about the future and memories of the past, revealing the overlapping nature of time in the narrative.

Florens's concern for multiple temporalities demonstrates that she sees not only time but also her subjectivity as liminal. She brings her relationships with her mother; Lina; Widow Ealing, Daughter Jane, and the villagers; and the blacksmith together when making her final declarations about identity: "You are correct. A minha mãe too. I am become wilderness but I am also Florens. In full. Unforgiven. Unforgiving. No ruth, my love. None. Hear me? Slave. Free. I last" (A Mercy 189). According to Montgomery, who argues that Florens "evolves throughout her perilous journey in ways that encourage a rethinking of colonial inscriptions of time, space, and identity" (628), Florens occupies a liminal subject position—she becomes one with the "wilderness"—because she abandons her search for a relational identity: "Because she self-identifies with natural world, not the social conventions of Early American society, she no longer experiences the fragmentary split that once characterized her life. It is from this empowered, self-defined position that Florens addresses her story to the nameless blacksmith" (634). In addition to tying her to the natural world, however, Florens's words on the final pages bring together her ties to multiple mother figures. Accordingly, she adopts both a liminal and relational identity. With her statement that she has "become wilderness," Florens joins her birthmother and the blacksmith, who call her "wild," with Lina, who once taught her "how to shelter in wilderness" (A Mercy 4, 166, 49). She also brings in her interaction with the villagers, since these men and women spurred her understanding of herself as a "small, feathered and toothy"—or wild—being (A Mercy 135).

While each of these interactions initially causes Florens to feel like she is "a thing apart" (A Mercy 135), her statements at the end of the novel reconcile her multiple selves and bring them in relation to others. Florens accepts her status as "wilderness," the identity that so many have foisted upon her, but she also claims her position as "Florens. In full" (A Mercy 189). This broader identity extends forward and backward throughout time, as evidenced by Florens's assertion, "I last." Instead of using the future tense and asserting, "I will last," Florens makes her statement of lasting identity—which has an historical origin but continues into the future—in the present tense. As Susmita Roye argues, Florens's "final words unambiguously expres[s] her intention to 'last,' to survive in the face of all reproofs and rejections" (221). Temporality and subjectivity overlap in a new way at the conclusion of the novel, as Florens carries the future idea of her identity into the present, joining it with her past experiences.

Florens additionally expresses a relational identity in the way she speaks about her narrative. She states that her words—the story of her past, present, and future—"[n]eed to fly up then fall, fall like ash over acres of primrose and mallow. Over a turquoise lake, beyond the eternal hemlocks, through clouds cut by rainbow and flavor the soil of the earth" (A Mercy 188). Although Florens and her mother attempt, as Montgomery argues, "to bridge the psychic, geographic, and linguistic gulf between Africa and the New World" with their messages to each other (629), Florens knows that her mother, like the blacksmith, "won't read her telling" (A Mercy 188). However, Florens does see her words as extending beyond death—her own and perhaps her mother's as well—and moving into a place of renewal, the "soil of the earth." In A Mercy, Morrison returns to the motif of the natural world's regeneration that she introduces in The Bluest Eye and carries forward to Beloved and beyond. Florens's statements about the soil echo, among other scenes, Sethe's excited imagining of what the spring will bring for her and Beloved (Beloved 201). Accordingly, the novel itself must be understood to occupy a liminal position, making links across time and space.

Multiple temporalities and identities, including the identity of Morrison's characters as well as the identity of her texts, converge as the reader takes responsibility for extending Florens's story into the future. While the villagers cast Florens out, her final understanding of herself and her message shows that she is not separate; she has a relational identity, and the reader joins her network of connections. Karavanta argues that the border crossings in A Mercy reveal "the future of other hybrid and marginal communities that will continue to haunt the national one and require representation and rights" (739). These communities rely on various forms of communication—from narratives rooted in the natural world to electronic texts complete with hashtags—to bring attention to their causes and signal their participation in larger relational networks. With each message sent, history moves into the future, and the present connects to the past, revealing not only what Morgenstern calls "the timeless time of trauma" but also the infinitude of activism (11).

CHAPTER 2

Posthuman Solidarity in
Sherley Anne Williams's *Dessa Rose*

In July of 2013, following the announcement of George Zimmerman's acquittal for the 2012 killing of seventeen-year-old Trayvon Martin in Sanford, Florida, the Twitter hashtag and movement #blacklivesmatter was born ("All"). From July 2013 to July 2014 tweets marked with the hashtag point out historical and contemporary instances of violence against unarmed black men and women, including Oscar Grant III and Renisha McBride, as well as the unequal treatment of black and white citizens who claim lawful use of deadly force under state stand-your-ground laws.[1] When video of Eric Garner repeating "I can't breathe" while restrained by New York City police officers prior to his death became public on July 17, 2014, and after news broke that Darren Wilson, a twenty-eight-year-old white police officer, fatally shot Michael Brown, an eighteen-year-old unarmed black man, in Ferguson, Missouri, on August 9, 2014, #blacklivesmatter gained new audiences. Activists began to chant the phrase at protests against state-sanctioned violence, and social media users increased their usage of the hashtag in Twitter, Facebook, Instagram, and Vine postings regarding police brutality, white privilege, and racial profiling.

As the name suggests, #blacklivesmatter speaks against the devaluing of black lives in white supremacist societies. However, members of other racial, ethnic, and national groups have rallied in support of the movement. In December of 2014, approximately seventy-five clergy members of various races and ethnicities joined individuals from the Black and Latino Caucus for a "die in" protest at New York City Hall. Following a similar protest the week before, Rabbi Jill Jacobs commented, "Rabbis and all Jews need to stand up and say that every single person is a creation in the divine image—that black lives matter" (Blumberg). Syracuse University students chanted "From Syracuse to Ferguson, black lives matter!" during a December 2014 multiracial march to protest the grand jury decision not to indict Wilson for Brown's death (O'Brien). The group Black Lives Matter Minnesota helped organize a protest involving individuals of multiple ethnicities that shut down part of the Mall of America during the 2014 holiday season ("Chanting"). In Ireland, England, France, and India, among other places, thousands of citizens from a variety of racial and ethnic groups have vocalized or otherwise displayed the slogans "black lives matter," "hands up, don't shoot," and "I can't breathe" as part of in-person and online protests to support Brown's and Garner's families and communities (Sharkey; Randhawa).[2] The ubiquity of #blacklivesmatter is also reflected in its selection of "word of the year for 2014" by the American Dialect Society, the first occurrence of a Twitter hashtag as winner (Schuessler), and its position (as Black Lives Matter rather than the hashtag) on the shortlist for *Time*'s 2015 Person of the Year (Altman). More recently, #blacklivesmatter leaders took the social media campaign to the White House, meeting with President Obama about civil rights (Cobb). Whether online, in print, or in person, #blacklivesmatter brings individuals from multiple social, cultural, and national groups together in solidarity to assert that black lives matter to black Americans as well as to members of other races from around the globe.

DIFFERENCES AND CONNECTIONS IN POSTHUMAN SUBJECTS AND SOCIETIES

The solidarity conveyed by various racial, ethnic, and religious groups involved in the #blacklivesmatter movement corresponds with the tenets of posthumanism, including the bringing together of disparate entities and, specifically, disparate subjects. Moments of contact between individuals from distinct racial, religious, or gender groups, for example, allow for the formation of posthuman communities through which people may work together against larger oppressive forces. The possibility of solidarity within posthuman communities reveals that intercultural understanding develops not from technological links specifically but our reliance on human and other connections, including during those moments in history often seemingly defined by separation.

Set during a particularly divisive time in American history—the antebellum period—Sherley Anne Williams's neo–slave narrative *Dessa Rose* (1986) demonstrates posthuman solidarity through the congruence of discourses and peoples set at odds by white supremacist and patriarchal forces. Williams's first novel tells the story of a young, pregnant, enslaved woman named Dessa Rose who evades a death sentence for her role in an uprising by joining other escaped slaves at a white woman's North Carolina farm. The physical, psychological, and rhetorical border crossings that occur within the novel, particularly as related to the intersection of black and white identities, incorporate the other as part of the self and, accordingly, diminish the power of white supremacy and patriarchy while preserving racial and gender differences. As such, the novel demonstrates the shift from power structures based in hierarchy to those founded in solidarity, the latter imbued with the potential to break down oppressive systems.

Posthuman theorists understand the subject as neither "discrete and sovereign" nor binary but as liminal, linked to multiple others along manifold lines of connection (Halberstam and Livingston 14). Rosi Braidotti states that the posthuman subject, like "figurations such as the feminist/the womanist/the queer/the cyborg/the diasporic," develops from the "processes of becoming" (164). "These processes," Braidotti argues, "assume that subject formation takes place in-between nature/technology; male/female; black/white; local/global; present/past—in the spaces that flow and connect the binaries" (164). Braidotti develops her theory of posthuman becoming from Deleuze and Guattari, who position becoming as a process that occurs within "assemblages," or the interconnection of distinct entities, "including all the attractions and repulsions, sympathies and antipathies, alterations, amalgamations, penetrations, and expansions that affect bodies of all kinds in their relations to one another" (Deleuze and Guattari 90). Furthermore, John Phillips and Jasbir K. Puar explain that Deleuze and Guattari's term *assemblage* derives from the French word *agencement*, "a term that means design, layout, organization, arrangement, and relations—the focus being not on content but on relations, relations of patterns" (Puar 57). The ongoing, relational process of becoming explains posthuman subjectivity as always already in flux, constituted by and constituting connected entities throughout space and time.

The continual development of the posthuman subject allows for new conceptions of individual identity—which must be seen as linked and liminal—as well as social and cultural identity categories. Drawing on Deleuze and Guattari's and Braidotti's discussions of becoming, Lauren J. Lacey argues that becoming shapes conceptions of race and gender. While Lacey focuses on the genre of fantastic fiction, her application of becoming to constructions of subjectivity and temporality within these texts establishes alternative modes of power for posthuman subjects: "The ethics of becoming [. . .] engenders awareness of potential and possibilities for alternative ways of acting/reacting to dominant and/or normative power structures. But such an ethics is only possible if subjectivity is understood as nomadic, both in time and in space" (71). Nomadic subjectivity, a term coined by Braidotti, emphasizes the multiplicity of the individual and "anchors the subject in an ethical bond to alterity, to the multiple and external others that are constitutive of that entity which, out of laziness and habit, we call the 'self'" (100). The nomadic or liminal nature of posthuman subjectivity requires that identity categories based on stable binaries be rethought.

While posthuman constructions of identity might seem irrelevant to real-life power systems with historical and cultural significance, such as the regime of white supremacy discussed above, posthuman subjectivities and communities can develop out of these binary-based systems, given that contemporary issues of difference and commonality originate in experiences of oppression. Judith Halberstam, Ira Livingston, and Alexander G. Weheliye likewise articulate the posthuman personality in terms of lived experiences of domination. In their introduction to *Posthuman Bodies*, Halberstam and Livingston position as posthuman those individuals who embrace as well as those who reject patriarchal, racist, and heteronormative systems, stating, "The posthuman marks a solidarity between disenchanted liberal subjects and those who were always-already disenchanted, those who seek to betray identities that legitimize or de-legitimize them at too high a cost. No one comes naturally to this conjecture; rather it must be continually forged within and among people and discourses" (9). By extending the idea of becoming—the continual and networked development of the subject—from posthuman individual identities to posthuman communal relationships, Halberstam and Livingston associate oppression, or at least "disenchantment," with all subjects in the posthuman society.

Weheliye further develops the concepts of community and solidarity Halberstam and Livingston introduce by investigating relationships among the disenfranchised in terms of racialization, "a conglomerate of socio-political relations that discipline humanity into full humans, not-quite-humans, and nonhumans" (*Habeas* 3), a system of categorization that, as Deleuze and Guattari assert, "operates by the determination of degrees of deviance in relation to the White-Man face" (Deleuze and Guattari 178). Weheliye, expanding an idea of community that can be traced back to

Donna Haraway's conception of the cyborg, allows that solidarity can occur between oppressed racial and ethnic groups if, for example, we consider their positions in hierarchical systems "in relational terms rather than through the passages of comparison, deviance, exception, or particularity" (*Habeas* 13). He goes on to argue, "While we should most definitely bring into focus the relays betwixt and between the genocide of indigenous populations in the Americas, the transatlantic slave trade, Asian American indentured servitude, and Latino immigration among many factors, we cannot do so in the grammar of comparison, since this will merely reaffirm Man's existent hierarchies rather than design novel assemblages of relation" (Weheliye, *Habeas* 13). Although he warns that subjects situated in relation risk reproducing hierarchical systems, Weheliye joins Halberstam and Livingston in suggesting the empowering potential of subjects joined in communities, a theory of solidarity articulated more fully and for the first time here (*Habeas* 46–47).

The theory of posthuman solidarity rests on the premise that posthuman societies—like individual posthuman subjects—develop out of and maintain a commitment to both difference and connection. Many theorists explore the posthuman subject as connected to and constituted by others, but what happens when we consider communities made up of multiple posthuman subjects, which, given the posthuman subject's interconnectivity to surrounding elements, seems a necessary precondition of posthumanity rather than a theoretical possibility? Rather than erasing difference, the posthuman subject and society speak to a solidarity that thrives on differences being put in conversation with one another. Posthuman solidarity develops when subjects within or across societies embrace individuality and work together to overcome systems that seek to hierarchize differences.

Although a theorist committed to humanism, Weheliye raises the question of posthuman communities in his scholarship on solidarity. Weheliye considers racial, ethnic, and religious groups who suffer in solidarity, but rather than understanding solidarity as a means of traditionally fighting oppression, he argues that bringing these groups together may "offer pathways to distinctive understandings of suffering that serve as the speculative blueprint for new forms of humanity, which are defined above all by overdetermined conjurings of freedom" (*Habeas* 14). Weheliye moves away from contemporary understandings of freedom, including "recognition based on the alleviation of injury or redressed by the laws of the liberal state," but he acknowledges that new types of freedom have "not (yet) [been] described," even in his book (*Habeas* 14–15).

Posthuman solidarity may signal pathways for both traditional and new freedoms for the oppressed. Weheliye's proposal that various racial, ethnic, and religious groups be considered together in terms of their shared experiences of suffering extends backward to the antebellum period in America. In bringing together those oppressed by white supremacist and patriarchal forces, Williams's *Dessa Rose* expresses posthuman solidarity. Although, as Tim A. Ryan, Ann Trapasso, Donna Haisty Winchell, and Joycelyn K. Moody argue, the relationships between black and white subjects in the neo–slave narrative contain "romanticized elements" (Ryan 160), evidence of posthuman solidarity in Williams's fictionalized history points to contemporary strategies for dismantling oppressive hierarchies.

POSTHUMAN SOLIDARITY IN DESSA ROSE

The novel *Dessa Rose* allows for the possibility that relationships rooted in difference—relationships among people of different races and genders, for example—can be understood according to solidarity rather than hierarchy. Considering the relationships in the novel, particularly the connection shared by Dessa Rose, a black woman, and Ruth "Rufel" Sutton, a white woman, in terms of posthuman theory reveals how Williams's characters' solidarity weakens the systems of white supremacy and patriarchy. This new theory of posthuman solidarity indicates that even within hierarchical systems, relational theories of the subject and community indicate a path by which hierarchies can be destroyed.

Posthuman solidarity presents itself in Williams's novel through the depiction of liminal black and white identities. The primary women characters in *Dessa Rose*, Dessa and Rufel, intersect in a way that emphasizes their bonds and, importantly, those forces they unite against. Readers first see evidence of the links between Dessa and Rufel and the liminality of black and white identities when Dessa arrives on the North Carolina farm, disoriented from her journey out of imprisonment and slavery and the recent birth of her son. She wakes briefly to see Rufel breastfeeding her daughter, Clara, whom Dessa identifies as "a year old, maybe, or more, with plump white arms and legs, wisps of light-colored hair on its smooth white head" (*Dessa* 88). As Dessa fades in and out of sleep, the scene in front of her changes. She "open[s] her eyes" to discover the "white woman, the shoulder still bare, the curly black head and brown face of a new baby nestled at her breast" (*Dessa* 88). The new baby, Dessa's son, Mony, takes sustenance from Rufel before suckling at his mother's breast, which links not only the white and black children—who, from Dessa's disoriented point of view, swap places seamlessly—but also the white and black women who feed them. While Dessa abhors the thought of Rufel feeding her son, she reluctantly admits the necessity of Rufel's breast milk when her own supply decreases. With Rufel acting as wet nurse to Mony and, later, Dessa serving as caretaker to Clara, the women overlap in their mothering by working together to meet their babies' physical and emotional needs.

In *Dessa Rose*, mothers transcend racial hierarchies and personal differences to care for their children, a community-focused action that ties into posthuman becoming and solidarity. The process of becoming indicative to posthuman subjectivity indicates that posthuman communities emerge from the intersection of subjects from different racial, ethnic, religious, or other backgrounds, and solidarity occurs when the subjects work toward similar goals. Halberstam and Livingston explain that while the human subject "functions to domesticate and hierarchize difference within the human (whether according to race, class, gender) and to absolutize difference between the human and the nonhuman"—"the human" functioning as a category from which, Weheliye clarifies, the black subject has been banned (*Habeas* 3, 8)—the posthuman subject thrives on the bringing together of differences (Halberstam and Livingston 10). The liminal posthuman subject does not erase differences, Halberstam and Livingston state, but lives between and among them, a relational configuration that allows for the possibility of not only posthuman subjects but also posthuman societies.

The relational quality of posthuman subjectivity necessitates the location of the individual into posthuman societies, yet the empowering potential of posthuman communities depends on the organization of the subjects within. Deleuze and Guattari argue that multiplicity—what we can understand as a building block of the posthuman subject and society—has no origin point from which it develops nor unity toward which it strives; rather, organizing forces are external, since "[m]ultiplicities are defined by the outside: by the abstract line, the line of flight or deterritorialization according to which they change in nature and connect with other multiplicities" (9). Because contemporary and historical posthuman communities exist not in a vacuum but, rather, in hierarchically organized societies, the empowering potential of posthuman communities must be considered in terms of those societies that shape them and which, as connected entities, they shape as well. In his understanding of assemblages, Weheliye likewise focuses on the influence of hierarchies, noting that the networked multiplicities "ought not be cognized as unavoidably positive or liberating, particularly when set against putatively rigid structures such as race and colonialism, since assemblages transport potential territorializations as often if not more frequently than lines of flight" (*Habeas* 47). Although "[a]ssemblages are inherently productive, entering into polyvalent becomings to produce and give expression to previously nonexistent realities, thoughts, bodies, affects, spaces, actions, ideas, and so on," posthuman conjunctions can reproduce oppressive hierarchical regimes, especially when made within said power structures (Weheliye, *Habeas* 46–47).

Accordingly, a solidarity-focused view of the posthuman community requires the rejection of the hierarchical systems that categorize and rank individuals. Contemporary conceptions of difference situate gender identities, for example, "in a binary machine that privileges heterosexual family formations" and erase other, more complex understandings of the gendered or sexed subject (Braidotti 99). In an effort to disentangle the subject from hierarchical systems, Braidotti champions the preservation of differences and the intersectionality of oppositional elements. Braidotti argues that posthuman theorists must "reassert the concept of difference as both central and non-essentialistic," given that the subject forms out of the "irrepressible flows of encounters, interactions, affectivity and desire, which one is not in charge of" (100). If the posthuman subject exists in a liminal space and time between and among differences, the concept of difference can be viewed through the lens of commonality rather than hierarchy. Considering difference within not only the posthuman subject but also the posthuman community in terms of commonality and solidarity allows those subjects oppressed by hierarchy—arguably, all subjects, even those in positions of power—to reconfigure their relationships with one another.

In Williams's novel, posthuman solidarity emerges out of the conjunction of the unique histories and experiences that Dessa and Rufel bring to their relationship. By sharing the role of mother yet maintaining their personal and cultural identities, Dessa and Rufel form a posthuman community. Moody argues that Williams's *Dessa Rose*, like Morrison's *Beloved*, depicts "self-esteem" growing "out of the affirmation of the self by others" (646). A posthumanist view of the novel further reveals that a community achieves empowerment through, in part, the maintenance of difference. Williams's frequent references to whiteness and blackness preserve the women's differences and allow readers to consider the characters in terms of liminality and solidarity rather than merely similarity. In the same scenes where she interchanges Dessa and Rufel in the role of mother, Williams positions their bodies as dissimilar. For Dessa, Rufel's pale skin contrasts with her dark surroundings: "a white woman *white* stared at her from the shadows of some room" (*Dessa* 82). Conversely, Rufel notes Dessa's darkness, viewing her as "a sooty blur against the whiteness of the pillow" (*Dessa* 97) and "a vivid chocolate and jet against the whiteness of the sheets" (*Dessa* 139). Both Dessa and Rufel perform the mother function, yet each woman sees the other as different from herself and distinct from her environment.

As *Dessa Rose* demonstrates, connections define the posthuman subject, but if sociopolitical forces organize those connected entities hierarchically, a posthuman community will reproduce oppressive power structures. In Williams's novel, the juxtaposition of character and environment, although expressed by each woman, carries different weight in white and black communities. Rufel positions Mony's "utter brownness" as "a striking contrast with the pallor of [her children's] skins" (*Dessa* 128), an observation about the unique color values of the children's skin tones that reflects the unequal social values ascribed to the children's membership in white supremacist society. Dessa likewise comments on the dissimilarities of black and white bodies, but she directly acknowledges the political implications of racial difference. Thinking about Nathan's black body in Rufel's bed, Dessa states, "Nathan sprawled in whiteness, white sheets, white pillows, white bosom. All he did was make them look whiter. He wasn't nothing but a mark on them. That's what we was in white folks' eyes, nothing but marks to be used, wiped out. [. . .] I couldn't trust all we had to something could swallow us like so many drops" (*Dessa* 171–72). Dessa comments on the physical characteristics of black and white skin and also the sociopolitical implications of the different skin tones. The idea of Rufel's white bed and body "swallowing" Nathan's blackness reflects Dessa's knowledge that the ruling white power controls and consumes black bodies.

However, even in the discussion of skin color, the novel demonstrates the dual possibility of the breakdown of hierarchies and the preservation of difference. Dessa asserts, "She [Rufel] did know the difference between black and white; I give her that. She wasn't that foolish. But where white peoples look at black and see something ugly, something hateful, she saw color" (*Dessa* 170). Rufel's recognition of color divorced from a ranking of value indicates a potential solidarity between blacks and whites in the novel. Although Dessa dismisses Rufel's role as an ally in her next breath, her differentiation of Rufel from other white people serves as evidence that Rufel rejects some white supremacist principles. Dessa's comments show that Rufel maintains an awareness of difference yet breaks down the hierarchical organization of whites and blacks.

The historical posthuman community depicted on Rufel's plantation, called Sutton's Glen or simply the Glen—a community characterized by the conjunction of disparate entities—shows that Williams's *Dessa Rose* condemns sociopolitical systems that organize multiplicities into hierarchies. Specifically, the novel critiques systems of racialization that mark black Americans as "nonhuman" as well as those hierarchies that position white and black women as "not-quite-human" and "nonhuman," respectively (Weheliye, *Habeas* 3). Although the black Dessa and the white Rufel rarely get along, they fight together against the white supremacist and patriarchal forces that constrain their lives. Once Dessa and Rufel begin to understand their experiences of oppression reflexively, they break down hierarchies in their relationship and society.

Thinking about the links between distinct forms of oppression allows differences to be considered in terms of solidarity rather than hierarchy. Although Weheliye focuses specifically on racial, ethnic, and religious groups and excludes gender groupings, he asserts that disenfranchised subjects and the individual "acts of aggression" they commit against ruling powers can be understood to operate according to a theory of solidarity: "Part of this project is to think the question of politically motivated acts of aggression in relational terms rather than through the passages of comparison, deviance, exception, or particularity, since they fail to adequately describe how specific instances of the relations that compose political violence realize articulations of an ontological totality: the constitutive potentiality of a totality structured in dominance composed of the particular processes of bringing-into-relation" (*Habeas* 13). Weheliye considers victims of sociopolitical violence in a new system of association based on solidarity, since traditional hierarchical systems serve to substantiate dominant powers that "as a general rule, only grant a certain number of exceptions access to the spheres of full humanity, sentience, citizenship, and so on" typically afforded to the ruling class (*Habeas* 13–14). Like Braidotti's posthuman nomadic figurations, Weheliye's "processes of bringing-into-relation" allow for an understanding of communities as composed of distinct but interconnected subjects, an idea of multiplicity linked to posthuman subjectivity and solidarity.

The solidarity that exists within Williams's *Dessa Rose* reveals that the posthuman subject's and community's rejection of damaging hierarchies has historical foundations as well as future applications. The novel as a whole, with its antebellum setting, reflects the historical underpinnings of posthuman solidarity. Additionally, the discussion of personal pasts— particularly the characters' childhoods—within the novel indicates that solidarity develops out of individual as well as national histories. Rufel and Dessa associate their role in childcare and their own positions as daughters with their relationship to "mammy," a figure who links the two women and signals their positioning along a posthuman liminal continuum. Ashraf H. A. Rushdy writes that the signifier *mammy* is one "both women feel entitled to use to describe their relationships to an earlier presence and a preceding generation" (*Neo-Slave* 154). When breastfeeding Mony, Rufel "imagine[s] herself saying to Mammy," the black mother figure who raised her from the age of thirteen, "'Well, I couldn't have them bringing a bleeding colored gal in where Timmy and Clara [Rufel's children] were having breakfast,' wheedling a little, making light" (*Dessa* 95). Rufel's impulse to justify her choice to mother a black child to the black woman who mothered her indicates that despite her ingrained racism, Rufel is capable of relating to others through bonds of affinity rather than hierarchy.

Dessa similarly evinces black and white solidarity through her recollections of her birthmother or "mammy" (spelled using a lower-case *m*), named Rose, during times when she is mothering or being mothered by others—including the white Rufel. Dessa first introduces readers to her mammy when convalescing in Rufel's bed. While Dessa initially believes she dreams of a white woman with hair "the color of fire" while lying in the slave quarters with mammy, she comes to recognize "the Quarters had been a dream" and Rufel, rather than mammy, is her reality (*Dessa* 86). As Rufel takes the place of mammy in Dessa's waking life—helping to care for Mony and swindle money that buys Dessa and her son passage to the West—the women forge a connection based on interdependence, or a posthuman solidarity in difference.

Dessa and Rufel do not merely share remembrances of their mammies: both women confuse the two mothers, eliding them into a single mother figure and, accordingly, positioning themselves as adoptive or figurative sisters. Although Rushdy asserts that "Williams takes pains to stress that neither Dessa nor Rufel is confused; each realizes that the other is talking about a different person" ("Reading" 375), Williams links the two mammies together in order to emphasize the developing bond between Dessa and Rufel. As a sleepy Dessa listens to Rufel drone on about her mammy while feeding Mony, Dessa wonders how she never knew about Rufel: "No white woman like this had ever figured in mammy's conversations, Dessa thought drowsily. And this would have been something to talk about: dinner and gowns—not just plain dresses" (Dessa 117). Rufel continues talking about Mammy dressing her until Dessa interrupts, asserting, "Wasn't' no 'mammy' to it. [. . .] Mammy ain't made you nothing!" (Dessa 118). The two women fight about Mammy/mammy until they realize that each had a relationship with a different mother. However, the confusion and comingling of Mammy/mammy—and, accordingly, Dessa and Rufel—persists throughout the novel. After she confesses to herself that "[o]f course" she and Dessa "were talking about two different people," Rufel wonders if Dessa could be the daughter of her mammy, named Dorcas, and she asks Harker about the women's connection (Dessa 121, 129–33). Rufel receives confirmation that Dorcas and Dessa are unrelated, yet she inquires several more times about their relationship (Dessa 137). Even once the women admit to each other the existence of two distinct mammies, Rufel and Dessa continue to overlap through their shared link to their individual mothers. Rufel tells Dessa, "Your mammy birthed you, and mines, mines just helped to raise me. But she loved me, [. . .] she loved me, just like yours loved you" (Dessa 154). While Dorcas's status as slave calls into question the validity of Rufel's assertion, Rufel's belief that Dorcas loved her "just like" Dessa's mother loved her own daughter shows that despite the racial hierarchy that separates Rufel and Dessa, a daughterly solidarity bonds the women.[3] Dessa and Rufel come together in relational rather than hierarchical terms by sharing their love for their mothers.

In addition to sharing a personal relationship, Rufel and Dessa, along with the escaped men and women at Sutton's Glen, develop solidarity through their response to the patriarchal and white supremacist social structures that constrain their lives. Rufel, Dessa, and the others work together to defraud slave buyers and earn money for their passage out of North Carolina. Rufel hopes the move will free her from her husband's rule—a threat that looms even in his absence—as well as the socioeconomic-related prejudice of her neighbors, while Dessa and her friends anticipate that traveling west will secure their freedom. When Dessa expresses anxiety about Rufel's involvement in the plan, Harker assures Dessa "this deal benefit her [Rufel] same as it do us" and that "she do got some stake in doing right by us" (*Dessa* 182). Rufel's "stake" may relate to her sexual relationship with Nathan—Harker tells Dessa, "Maybe she wouldn't do it just for the money" (*Dessa* 188)—but readers come to understand that her stake also emerges out of her empathetic association with Dessa, Harker, Nathan, and the other runaway slaves.

The novel supports the notion that shared experiences not only bond the black and white inhabitants of Sutton's Glen but also break down conventional racial hierarchies on the farm. The Glen's remote location—geographically, as the house sits away from neighboring properties, and socially, as Rufel's poverty makes her an unwelcome associate to nearby whites—reflects Rufel's subordinate position in the North Carolina social hierarchy. Moreover, on Rufel's farm, black men and women possess knowledge, skills, and numbers that invalidate Rufel's authority. In the absence of Rufel's husband, the black workers at the Glen, namely Mammy and Harker, become leaders in the home and on the farm. Williams writes, "Rufel had been uneasy as the suggestions [for what to plant and when] diverged more and more from Bertie's practices, but Mammy, citing as justification the experience of the new darky, Harker, who had wandered into the Glen sometime during the winter, had easily quieted Rufel's hesitant questioning. She was baffled by the larger questions of crop management that were implicit in these changes and found it easier in this, as in so much else, to rely on Mammy's judgment" (*Dessa* 112). The escaped slaves at the Glen serve not as advisors to Rufel, ceding to her rule, but instead as authorities, making decisions about what happens and when. The black men and women share their talents with the white Rufel, who shares her land with them. As Nathan tells Dessa, the people at Sutton's Glen develop a relationship built on mutual benefit and trust: "We *been* trusting her all along, just like *she* been trusting us" (*Dessa* 189). Those living on the plantation deconstruct traditional hierarchies, and the Glen functions as a liminal space, a place where those suffering racial, gender, or class oppression come together and create a new system of relation.

While top-down power structures crumble at the Glen, moments of contact between disparate subjects in the novel do not necessarily destroy hierarchies; instead, new hierarchical systems may develop. Weheliye's theory of assemblages corroborates this possibility: "While thinking through the political and institutional dimensions of how certain forms of violence and suffering are monumentalized and others are relegated to the margins of history remains significant, their direct comparison tends to lead to hierarchization and foreclose further discussion" (*Habeas* 13). In other words, rather than the destruction of hierarchies, assemblages of disparate parts may reproduce old or produce new hierarchies. In his analysis of *Dessa Rose*, Rushdy argues that the Glen reproduces old systems of relation, stating that although Rufel does not own the escaped slaves at the Glen, "she maintains remarkable control over their narratives" (*Neo-Slave* 153). However, once Rufel makes links between her relationship with Dorcas and Dessa's relationship with Rose—that is, as she develops as a posthuman subject who develops through manifold lines of connection—her "desire for controlling the black Others in her life becomes somewhat less urgent" (Rushdy, *Neo-Slave* 158). Rufel's realization reveals that new systems of relation can form within hierarchical power structures, though ladders of power threaten to resurface.

In addition to shaping the larger social structure at the Glen, Dessa and Rufel's weakening of the hierarchies that threaten their personal relationship allows them to fight together against oppressive social and political forces. Moody argues that Dessa's "reclaiming of herself in her fugitive slave status depends on a supportive community," including the men she escaped the coffle with and the black and white women at Sutton's Glen, "most especially Ruth" (644). Although the two women engage in rhetorical battles throughout the novel, they rely on each other to survive when traveling through the South to con slave traders. Michele Wallace asserts that through her depiction of Dessa and Rufel's "friendship," Williams gives her readers a view "into the world that black and white women shared in the antebellum South," a world where exists—at least in the fiction writer's imagination—the potential of "collective struggle that ultimately transcends the stumbling-blocks of race and class" (145). During their tour of the South, the two women gain consciousness of their "collective struggle" during their encounter with the sexually aggressive Mr. Oscar. Dessa helps Rufel escape from Mr. Oscar during an intended nighttime sexual assault, and the two women bond over their shared vulnerability: "The white woman was subject to the same ravishment as me," Dessa thinks. "I hadn't knowed white mens could use a white woman like that, just take her by force same as they could with us" (*Dessa* 201). She continues, "I never will forget the fear that come on me when Miz Lady called me on Mr. Oscar, that *knowing* that she was as helpless in this as I was, that our only protection was ourselfs and each others" (*Dessa* 202). Dessa's preservation of "us" and "them" language to distinguish her struggles from Rufel's maintains the integrity of distinct black and white experiences of gender oppression, yet her statements of comparison—"the same ravishment as me," "same as they could with us," "she was as helpless in this as I was"—unite the two women in solidarity. Moreover, Dessa's assertion that she and Rufel must work together, that their only recourse against sexual violence comes from "ourselfs and each other," reveals that the two women, to use Weheliye's words, "design novel assemblages of relation" by which they express the destructive power of "Man's existent hierarchies," including patriarchy (*Habeas* 13). Despite the different goals and hardships of Dessa and Rufel, their shared experiences of subjugation allow them to join together against tyrannical sociopolitical forces.

Williams further demonstrates solidarity between black and white characters in the novel by rhetorically linking statements of care between Dessa and Rufel with statements of care among those of a single race. After working with Rufel to defeat Mr. Oscar, Dessa realizes that her negative opinion of Rufel shifts: "You can't do something like this with someone and not develop some closeness, some trust" (*Dessa* 206). Dessa's thoughts of "some closeness, some trust" echo the sentiments Nathan articulates when explaining to Rufel the bond shared by the runaway slaves: "us three—we did it [escaped] and we made it. It's gots to be some special feeling after that" (*Dessa* 149). Dessa expresses a similar connection with those who escaped the coffle, asserting, "Nathan and Cully, and Harker, too, had risked something for me and I felt bound to them—and them to me—as tight as blood-kin" (*Dessa* 174–75). Although she initially states that Rufel "wasn't no part of that knot; the only way she could get in was to loosen it" (*Dessa*

175), the experience the women share the night of Mr. Oscar's aggressions allows Dessa to see them as "partnered" and perhaps even "friends" (*Dessa* 219). Dessa and Rufel, like Dessa and the formerly enslaved men, shift from a relation based in hierarchy—whether race or gender oriented—to a bond situated in solidarity.

Williams's novel shows that although the weakening of the racial hierarchy in Dessa and Rufel's relationship affects how the women see each other and how they view race relations outside of their community at Sutton's Glen, larger race and gender hierarchies remain intact. As Weheliye states in his assessment of Stuart Hall's conception of articulation, which "emphasizes relational connectivity," assemblages must be considered in terms of historical power structures, including hierarchical social relations, which may "territorialize" assemblages and reproduce dominant social structures: "Articulated assemblages such as racialization materialize as sets of complex relations of articulations that constitute an open articulating principle—territorializing and deterritorializing, interested and asubjective—structured in political, economic, social, racial, and heteropatriarchal dominance" (*Habeas* 48–49). In Williams's novel the assemblage of black and white subjects within a white supremacist and patriarchal society simultaneously maintains and deconstructs existent hierarchies. In Dessa's recollection of their relationship, Rufel projects her empathetic bond with the escaped slaves outward, expressing that "if white folks knew slaves as she knew [Dessa and the others], wouldn't be no slavery. She thought that was what'd ruined her husband—seeing how much money you could make if you owned other peoples. This is why she felt slavery was wrong, because peoples was no more to you than a pair of hands, stock, sometimes not even a name" (*Dessa* 211). Rufel's understanding of the Glen's inhabitants as people rather than property, combined with her earnest belief that other whites would likewise share her view "[i]f they just knew" (*Dessa* 212), shows that she imagines race-based differences in terms of solidarity rather than hierarchy. However, Rufel's position of racial privilege prevents her from recognizing, as Dessa and her friends do, that action must accompany belief in order for hierarchies to be destroyed. Dessa states, "I couldn't understand how she could watch white folks buying up our peoples right and left and say this. As far as white folks not knowing how bad slavery was—they was the ones made it, was the ones kept it. Master could've freed me anytime and I wouldn't've never said him nay" (*Dessa* 212). Dessa notes that while Rufel's interactions with her changed the white woman's view of slavery, most whites do not form empathetic bonds with their slaves, or if they do, they fail to act empathetically, and white supremacy continues to reign.

Indeed, the moments of solidarity between Dessa and Rufel do not erase the larger social hierarchy that exists due to their racial difference. Following the encounter with Mr. Oscar, both Rufel and Dessa arm themselves with hatpins for use against lascivious men. However, Rufel possesses a bigger and more readily available weapon than what she gives to Dessa (*Dessa* 202–03). The fact, first, that Dessa keeps a hatpin on her person only because Rufel buys Dessa the weapon and, second, that Rufel holds a larger hatpin, one visible to the public and more easily within reach, reveals Rufel's position of power over Dessa and, perhaps, Rufel's belief that the threat of sexual violence against her takes precedence over the sexual violence faced by Dessa. Biman Basu argues that the "possibility of Rufel's regression into the law of the father"—the patriarchal power structure of slavery and white supremacy—"constantly threatens to disrupt" the solidarity-based system of relation developed among the travelers (105). The mutually beneficial, empathetic association between Dessa and Rufel cannot, as Basu asserts, "be entirely abstracted and severed from the political economy and from the larger social-political-economic complex," and Rufel's performance threatens to reproduce the power structure she purports to reject (106). In order for solidarity to replace hierarchy, Basu argues, "power relations [. . .] will have to be rigorously negotiated. And the practice of living will have to be formulated in terms of competent practice" (111). For differences to be organized nonhierarchically in posthuman communities, empathetic intent must be matched with empathetic action.

The shifting nature of the solidarity between Dessa and Rufel—at times their relationship breaks down local hierarchies, while at other points the novel's assemblages of black and white subjects reinforce white supremacy and patriarchy—reflects the fluidity of posthuman bonds: the continual development of the subject along networks of relation means that identity and community always already exist in a state of transition. While the novel does not demonstrate the destruction of hegemonic structures—and, of course, it could not, given that it takes place during the historical period of slavery, a time followed by centuries of ongoing oppression against people of color as well as (and including) women—Weheliye argues that thinking about assemblages in terms of total freedom limits their potential: "Why are formations of the oppressed deemed liberatory only if they resist hegemony and/or exhibit the full agency of the oppressed? What deformations of freedom become possible in the absence of resistance and agency?" (*Habeas* 2). Moving beyond white humanist conceptions of resistance and agency, Weheliye poses the question of "what different modalities of the human come to light if we do not take the liberal humanist figure of Man as the master-subject but focus on how humanity has been imagined and lived by those subjects excluded from this domain?" (*Habeas* 8). If we read Williams's novel not according to resistance and agency, then, but in terms of Weheliye's suggested new modes of the human—alternatively conceived as the posthuman—then the potential of fluid networks of relations becomes clearer.

When read according to posthumanism, Williams's novel depicts bonds based in solidarity as well as hierarchy, a proposition that positions power systems, like the individuals who construct them, as temporal and fluid constructions. The ease with which Rufel, Dessa, and the others at Sutton's Glen assume positions in the existing power hierarchy in order to swindle money from white slave traders shows that the components of the system are constructed and changeable. Rufel, in the guise of a slave owner, sells Harker, Ned, Castor, and Flora, who masquerade as her slaves. Nathan drives the wagon, and Dessa, in the role of nursemaid, minds Rufel's daughter (*Dessa* 193–94). The light-skinned, mixed-race Cully stays behind at the farm in the character of Rufel's white brother from Charleston (*Dessa* 59, 194–95). Each of these performances—owner, slave, driver, nursemaid, and brother—reflects an accepted social position of the individual who plays it: Rufel was a slave owner; Harker, Ned, Castor, Flora, and Nathan were slaves; Dessa, like her mammy and Rufel's mammy, provides care and comfort for children; and Cully serves as surrogate brother to the orphans on Rufel's farm. Whether the characters formerly or currently identify with the roles they occupy, their ability to shift in and out of their parts in the scheme reveals the performative and, therefore, fluid aspects of race and gender, as well as their related hierarchies. As Judith Butler argues, the "shifting and contextual phenomenon" of gender exists as "a relative point of convergence among culturally and historically specific sets of relations" (14). Gender, like race and other assemblages, must be understood as provisional in that it operates according to the temporally specific context into which individuals produce and reproduce it.

Williams's novel demonstrates that even the role of slave, where a failed (or successful) performance can result in death, never becomes natural for those who occupy it. Moreover, Dessa and her cohort understand that race itself is a construction. While playing lady's maid to Rufel, Dessa fails to respond when Mr. Oscar calls her out of her name and commands her with the identifier "Nigger." Looking back on this event, Dessa reminds herself, "I was slave; I was 'nigger'; I couldn't forget that for the rest of the journey" (*Dessa* 198). Dessa pairs the rejected name *Nigger* with the metonym *slave*, suggesting that neither term describes her accurately. Despite spending most of her life in servitude and capitulating to Rufel's racial authority several times while at the farm, Dessa views the role of slave, the position at the bottom of the antebellum social hierarchy, as a performance. As Morrison reminds us, racism exists as a "construct" (Interview), and despite the fact that black and, to a lesser extent, white lives depend upon successful performances of racial identities, Williams's novel never fails to remind readers of the temporality of race- and gender-based hierarchies.

Understanding hierarchies as located in specific places and times does not make the lived experiences of those subjects positioned hierarchically any less oppressive. However, the fluid nature of power relations allows for the imagining of differences organized according to solidarity rather than hierarchy. William's *Dessa Rose* ends in a place of liminality, where subjects from different backgrounds and racial groups overlap and intersect yet remain distinct entities. Dessa and Rufel, "by the sheer competence of their performance" of slave and mistress roles (Basu 110), enable Dessa to escape from Adam Nehemiah, a white writer working on a book about slave uprisings who desires to see Dessa punished for fleeing prison and evading her death sentence. While Nehemiah equates Dessa and Rufel because of their shared gender—"You-all in this together," he tells them, "womanhood. [. . .] All alike. Sluts" (*Dessa* 232)—the novel allows the women to act in solidarity while maintaining their subjective integrity. In the novel's final spoken conversation, the words of Rufel and Dessa intersect, yet two distinct lines of commentary run through the paragraph: "'Ruth,' 'Dessa,' we said together; and 'Who was that white man—?' 'That was the white man—' and stopped. We couldn't hug each other, not on the streets, not in Arcopolis, not even after dark; we both had sense enough to know that. The town could even bar us from laughing; but that night we walked the boardwalk together and we didn't hide our grins" (*Dessa* 233). Dessa's statements overlap with Rufel's, but readers have no difficulty knowing who voices each line. The words mark Dessa and Rufel's defeat of the man who symbolizes white supremacy and patriarchy in the novel, and the utterances speak to the power of solidarity over hierarchy. As previously stated, the women do not erase racial or gender hierarchies—the novel ends with Dessa telling her descendants of her physical separation from Rufel—yet the book depicts the progress made, both in Dessa and Ruth's personal relationship and the larger social structure of black and white relations.

In *Dessa Rose*, subjective liminality and temporal liminality meet as Williams creates a contemporary novel based on two antebellum histories: one of a pregnant, enslaved woman who helped lead a coffle uprising in Kentucky in 1829, and the other of a white woman who housed runaway slaves in North Carolina in 1830. "How sad," Williams thought, upon discovering the two incidents, "that these two women never met" (Author's Note 5).[4] As Williams weaves the histories together, she also connects the subjectivities of the women, allowing the fictionalized Kentucky woman to shape the fictionalized North Carolina woman, and vice versa. Williams's Dessa and Rufel come together in the spaces between their distinct racial, cultural, and historical selves, and the novel demonstrates posthuman solidarity by linking those oppressed by white supremacist and patriarchal forces. While hierarchies do not disappear from Williams's novel, the bonds between disparate subjects reflect that connectivity, whether organized in hierarchy or solidarity, characterizes posthuman communities. The bonds forged across lines of race and gender in *Dessa Rose* speak to the origins of posthuman solidarity and the possibility that social relations can change. Other neo–slave narratives—including those found in songs and on the screen—similarly reveal that new expressions of subjectivity and community develop when the boundaries of self and other and past, present, and future blur.

Afrofuturist Aesthetics in the Works of Erykah Badu, Janelle Monáe, and Gayl Jones

In Sam Spratt's cover art for the standard and deluxe editions of Janelle Monáe's second studio album, *The Electric Lady* (2013), Monáe promotes the time-traveling power of Afrofuturism. Literally, she wears her ability to move among past, present, and future temporalities on her sleeve, or rather, her wrist, where she brandishes a barcode. According to the mythology associated with the album art, the "Digital Auction Code" displayed by Cindi Mayweather, Monáe's alter-ego, "denotes that she is FREE and NOT FOR SALE. She has become a Q.U.E.E.N., an E1 Class android superstar, with full manumission papers" ("Concerning").[1] The barcode and the mythos surrounding it signal the convergence of multiple time periods. The code recalls the histories of African slaves who were branded by their American "owners" and sold at markets and auctions. Additionally, the code points toward present and future times, not only due to its similarity to the barcodes, matrix codes, and microchips we see and scan daily but also for the information it provides about Mayweather, a free android associated with the Droid Rebel Alliance that seeks to disrupt the futuristic human-android hierarchy that echoes contemporary race, gender, sexuality, and class conflicts.

With her aural and visual blurring of the boundaries between self and other; human and android; and past, present, and future, Monáe joins musicians Sun Ra, George Clinton, and Erykah Badu and authors Samuel Delany and Octavia Butler as a member of the Afrofuturist elite. Afrofuturism, the cultural aesthetic of a specifically black posthumanism, contends that boundary crossings enable black subjects to connect to black history in the present and also find authority in the potentiality of the future. With this blurring of subjective and temporal boundaries, Afrofuturism endorses posthuman theory's embrace of liminality, a threshold state or experience of occupying two positions simultaneously. In songs like Monáe's "Q.U.E.E.N." (2013)—where mentions of Nefertiti, Harriet Tubman, and Marvin Gaye appear alongside references to "electric ladies" and "electric sheep" (a nod to

Philip K. Dick's 1968 android-abundant novel)—and Erykah Badu's "Window Seat" (2010)—which brings together a blues guitarist and a character from *Star Trek* with the lyrics, "On this porch I'm rockin' / Back and forth like Lightnin' Hopkins / If anybody speak to Scotty / Tell him, 'Beam me up'"—Afrofuturists reveal black identities and cultures as temporally flexible, grounded in the potential of the future as well as the power of the past.

Discussion of Afrofuturist liminality in songs by Monáe and Badu extends to works of historical fiction, such as Gayl Jones's blues-infused neo–slave narrative, *Corregidora* (1975). Monáe and Badu offer new spaces and places for fuller black expression by putting forward in their music, videos, and album art imagined black futures as well as alternative black histories. Jones similarly uses music in her novel to endorse an Afrofuturist or black posthumanist temporal liminality: her protagonist hears stories of and sings songs about the days of slavery in order to communicate that moving beyond the pain of the past requires an engagement with both black histories and futures. Although set in the past, contemporary neo–slave narratives such as Jones's *Corregidora* feature characters with a forward-looking perspective that allows them to conceive of their present and past circumstances as continually developing. These works of historical fiction, like Afrofuturist music and stories, participate in the black posthumanist project of finding personal and communal authority in the future as well as the past and present.

BLACK HUMANIST AND POSTHUMANIST
READINGS OF AFROFUTURIST MUSIC

Afrofuturist musicians, writers, filmmakers, and artists primarily concern themselves with creating black worlds. These worlds might contain recovered or alternative histories. They might function as politically charged commentaries on the present. They might set the stage for imagined futures. No matter the specific purpose, the worlds created by Afrofuturists tell the varied and variable stories of black people and cultures as they exist throughout—or between—time. Mark Dery, who coined the term *Afrofuturism* in the early 1990s, states that the black musicians, artists, and writers of the movement have "other stories to tell about culture, technology, and things to come" (182). Dery's reference to "other stories" acknowledges the existence of a history of stories, but his mention of "things to come" draws attention to the future. More than twenty years later, Afrofuturists continue to shed light on the relationship of black pasts, presents, and futures. Theorist and music journalist Kodwo Eshun ties the temporal connectivity or liminality of Afrofuturism to Paul Gilroy's spatial and subjective understanding of the Black Atlantic as a "rhizomorphic, fractal structure" (Gilroy, *Black* 4). Eshun links the scientific and technological rhetoric of Gilroy's definition to the "webbed networks" of communication that exist within the "digital diaspora" (*More* oo[–oo6]).[2] His assessment of Gilroy's language specifically joins the past (i.e., the *root*-like structure of the rhizome) to the present and future (i.e., digital webs of communication). The very language of Afrofuturist theorizing indicates that no understanding of black space, time, or identity—from Gilroy's Black Atlantic to Monáe's "black and white"—can be complete without an acknowledgment of liminality.

The Afrofuturist commitment to liminality presents itself most clearly in music. According to Ytasha L. Womack, a need to blur boundaries, a desire to "shif[t] the edge," defines the genre (56). "There are no barriers in Afrofuturist music," she states, "no entity that can't emit a rhythmic sound, no arrangements to adhere to, no locked-in structures about chorus and verse" (57). As this focus on freedom suggests, Afrofuturism remains suspicious of authentic histories and identities and favors, instead, the interstitial spaces between powers, cultures, subjectivities, and temporalities. While this interest in liminality distinguishes Afrofuturist music from other genres—Eshun initially asserts that Afrofuturist music does not emerge from a musical history but rather "arrives from the future" (*More* oo[–oo3], oo[–oo5])—embracing liminality means that Afrofuturist music must look forward and, as Eshun acknowledges in a later publication, backward as well ("Further" 289). Afrofuturist music thus develops out of that which comes after it and that which comes before, including the "unruly," "fluid," and "subversive" genres of blues and jazz (Grandt, *Kinds* xiv).

Considering Afrofuturist music alongside the jazz forebear specifically reveals how Afrofuturism's embrace of temporal liminality pervades even its ties to musical and other histories: both Afrofuturism and jazz demonstrate a commitment to creativity that can be linked to the future as well as the past. Jazz scholar Jürgen E. Grandt states that "jazz can be loosely defined as an art form pioneered and developed by African Americans that seeks to integrate freedom with structure, spontaneity with forethought, individual expression with collective interplay, West African musical residuals with certain European concepts and instruments" (*Kinds* xiii). For Grandt, jazz music's engagement with seemingly disparate elements such as freedom and structure extends to a larger "jazz aesthetic" that highlights the "hybridity" of black culture throughout time: "the 'blackness' of black culture, of both the music and the literature, in fact thrives on hybridity, harnessing the energies inherent in the tension-filled process of cultural product as well as simultaneously affirming the African American (literary) tradition" (*Kinds* xviii). Grandt points to the temporal interplay present in jazz music, the jazz aesthetic, and black culture as a whole when he makes note of the present- and future-located processes of production and the past-situated affirmation of tradition. However, he laments that not all critics acknowledge these boundary crossings:

> Literary criticism has tended to ignore or distort jazz's inherent hybridity in order to posit a program of authentic blackness—or, indeed, in order to eschew probing the relationship of whiteness to blackness. Jazz suggests that any notion about and expression of "authentic" blackness is a *process*, a process that, like jazz improvisation, occurs in time and therefore asks to be continuously negotiated anew. And precisely because an authentic blackness embedded in time must necessarily also react to impulses from "outside" the African American tradition, the resulting hybridity does not dilute authenticity, but it *is* that authenticity: the jazz aesthetic in fact encourages the usage of extraneous material, *as long as that material is brought into some sort of negotiation with the tradition's historical conscience*[. . .] . (*Kinds* 110)

According to Grandt, the achievement of black authenticity must be understood as a process that not only allows for difference but also incorporates difference into tradition, thereby altering the authentic black subject, the black tradition in which the subject belongs, and elements of difference the subject encounters. In this way, jazz hybridity and Afrofuturist liminality overlap: just as the future exists in a state of flux for each aesthetic, so do the past and present, as well as every entity that resides within these temporalities.

While both musical traditions recognize the mutability and interconnectivity of past, present, and future, the process of authentication prevalent in jazz music associates the genre with black humanism, a theory of identity and community that developed in response to a history of black oppression and the denial of black humanity. Theorists intertwine traditional notions of the human with the liberal humanist subject, a being characterized by self-control and self-determination (Macpherson 3). Despite the irrelevance of these qualities of humanity to women, people of color, the poor, and other groups denied independent personhood, many authors and critics of black music, art, film, and literature engage in what Eshun calls "a perpetual fight for human status, a yearning for human rights, a struggle for inclusion within the human species" (*More* 00[–006]). Theorists Alexander G. Weheliye and Marlo David likewise argue that black thought "has not evinced the same sort of distrust and/or outright rejection of 'man' in its universalist, post-Enlightenment guise as Western antihumanist or posthumanist philosophies" (Weheliye, "'Feenin'" 26). Because the humanity of the black subject has been denied during slavery and other times of oppression, many black authors work to create what Sylvia Wynter identifies as "different modalities of 'human being'" ("On Disenchanting" 243). Weheliye argues that these modes "incorporate the colonial and racialist histories of the 'human'" into black humanist notions of identity, which emphasize "the historicity and mutability of the 'human' itself, gesturing toward different, catachrestic, conceptualizations of this category" ("'Feenin'" 27, 26). Although critic Richard Iton questions the ability of certain words and concepts to become dissociated from embedded contexts and "hierarchical designs" (14), Weheliye asserts that, in the case of the human, revision occurs: if historically situated and made multiple, particular black "performances of the human" become disentangled from the white, liberal humanist tradition ("'Feenin'" 30). Accordingly, Weheliye finds that black humanists' contextualized, non-hegemonic understandings of humanity make the human a category worthy of ongoing consideration, one that he asks posthuman theorists to consider alongside their own readings of the black subject ("'Feenin'" 40).

The project of black humanism, which acknowledges both the hybridity (or "mutability," to quote Weheliye) and historicity of humanity in an effort to achieve an understanding of the black human subject, corresponds with the project that Grandt envisions those who embrace his jazz aesthetic will take up: the bringing together of the new and the old in order to determine a historically authentic—though always shifting—blackness. During their engagement with multiple, networked temporalities and identities—hallmarks of a posthumanist ontology—Afrofuturists draw on humanist projects by acknowledging the importance of black history without positing a single historical origin for authentic black identities. Eshun asserts that Afrofuturism "is concerned with the possibility for intervention within the dimension of the predictive, the projected, the proleptic, the envisioned, the virtual, the anticipatory and the future conditional" ("Further" 293). Eshun's comments, though centered on the movement's relationship to the future, signal the existence of liminal temporalities, since the future can "intervene" on the present and past. Afrofuturism's predictive, proleptic nature promotes not only liminal conceptions of time but also identity: as past, present, and future moments overlap, so do past, present, and future visions of blackness.

Acknowledging blackness as an identity in process requires that multiple temporalities be explored together. In his examination of "black authenticity," E. Patrick Johnson asserts that "the concept of blackness has no essence" but is, instead, "contingent on the historical, social, and political in terms of its production" (3). Manifold forces have shaped ideas of blackness throughout time; accordingly, even within Afrofuturist and posthumanist theorizing, which reject the privileging of history over other temporalities, using history as one of many reference points through which to understand the present allows for contextualized readings of black identity and community. Evaluating history in the search for black authenticity inspires critical engagement with constructions of blackness privileged in the present or anticipated for the future, since these constructions, like their antecedents, risk participating in exclusionary practices. Black narratives, such as those shared by Badu, Monáe, and Jones, function as "formerly unarticulated histories" (Rody 5) that work in the tradition of ethnic and postcolonial literatures and poststructuralist and postmodernist theories to destroy master narratives—such as that of the liberal humanist subject—and tell previously unheard or ignored tales. Acknowledging the "arbitrariness of authenticity" in these narratives prevents them from perpetuating the exclusionary practices of the master narratives they supplant (Johnson 3).

Similarly, considering posthumanist texts and the Afrofuturist aesthetic in the context of humanist (and other) histories works to ensure that posthuman theory does not adopt the exclusivity of certain humanisms. While posthumanist theorists Judith Halberstam and Ira Livingston determine history to be "inefficient as a method of processing information"—they argue that "[a]s history slows down relative to events in the realm of information and meaning, the future remains on hold" (3)—Carol Mason asserts that posthumanists should consider the past in their explorations of the future in order to understand the political implications of the very act of theorizing. She states, "I fear that without saying 'where we've been' and without defining specific political goals, even the best intentions [in theorizing the posthuman subject] can obscure the historical and discursive production of subjectivities, and consequently hide some of the political opportunities and pitfalls available in understanding such productions" (Mason 236). As Eshun, Weheliye, and Kalí Tal point out, this historical contextualization becomes especially important when considering theories concerned with identity, since ignoring the multiplicity of history can lead to privileging particular portions—or peoples—of the past.

The multiplicity of history as well as the relationship between historicity and futurity present themselves clearly in Afrofuturist music, including in songs and videos by Erykah Badu and Monáe. Each artist holds an important place in the Afrofuturist movement: Badu "emerged during Afrofuturism's formation and frequently drops imagery and references to quantum physics, motherships, and the revolution in her music and videos" (Womack 146), while Monáe has been dubbed Afrofuturism's "new pioneer," "new avatar," and "poster girl" (Calveri; Anders; Gonzales). Songs and videos from both women exemplify the time-traveling power of Afrofuturism, yet critics adopt a history-focused stance in regard to Badu, arguing that she connects her audience to an authentic past, and a future-focused position when considering Monáe, asserting that she brings her followers into a new tomorrow. However, considering the artists alongside one another confirms their shared commitment to temporal liminality.

Badu—who, as David notes, proclaims herself an "analog girl in a digital world" in her song "On & On" (David 697)—appears to be a singer and performer devoted to history, yet she embraces temporal liminality in her songs, album artwork, and personal style. Additionally, in her music videos she traverses different continents and time periods in order to transport black histories and futures into the present for the viewer. In the video for "Next Lifetime," a song from her 1997 album, *Baduizm*, Badu travels through Africa and North American during several lifetimes. In the 2011 video for "Gone Baby, Don't Be Long," featured on *New Amerykah Part Two (Return of the Ankh)*, released in 2010, Badu moves via conveyor belt through an animated world that references ancient Egyptian civilizations, the American Industrial Revolution, and technologically advanced futures. While these videos depict the continuity of past, present, and future, Badu rejects a singular, stagnant black history or identity by intertwining historically situated ideas of blackness with projections of black futures.

As Afrofuturist or black posthumanist pieces, Badu's songs and videos signal that our present ideas about black identity and even black history develop from visions of the future as well as knowledge of the past. However, Badu demonstrates humanist leanings as well, given her assertion of an authentic blackness. David argues that Badu's constantly shifting appearance "enforces a complex signification on concretized notions of embodied blackness through a series of reversals and ruptures while she simultaneously invokes a natural, authentic, essential black humanity that resonates within spaces of neo-soul identity" (698, 702). Badu's seemingly paradoxical rejection of "concretized notions of embodied blackness" and embrace of "a natural, authentic, essential black humanity" links her Afrofuturist music to jazz, which similarly presents the "expression of 'authentic' blackness" as "a process that [. . .] occurs in time and therefore asks to be continuously negotiated anew" (Grandt, *Kinds* 110). By directing her "gaze forward into the post-human/post-black future and back into the black humanist past simultaneously" (David 698), Badu refuses to determine a single historical origin point for authentic black identities, situating them as in-process instead.

The video for "Next Lifetime" relies on temporal liminality to emphasize the continuous negotiations involved in determining authentic blackness. While "Next Lifetime" closes in the year 3037, the cast of characters returns to the "Motherland" setting of the video's 1637 opening. Moreover, the costuming featured in the 3037 segment signals the continuation or return of history: the metallic face paint donned by the black men and women represents a futuristic aesthetic, but the 3037 robes and headdresses echo the clothing styles of the 1637 opening and the 1968 middle section. Badu further connects futurity and history through the cultural practices depicted in the video. Text overlay labels the event depicted in the 3037 piece an "ancient choosing ceremony," which not only acknowledges the significance of history—the "ancient" quality of the ceremony gives it weight in the 3037 present—but also the function of the future. Changes in costume color, for example, show that the movement of time has altered the ceremony, yet the participants fold these modifications into the ceremony without comment. The present and future, then, become part of "ancient" history.

In the Afrofuturist videos "Gone Baby, Don't Be Long" and "Next Life-time," among others, Badu exists as a liminal figure—an artist who, accord-ing to David, "performs in the breaks, in the gaps between essentialized blackness and post-soul possibility to project forward into future black-ness" (705). Similarly, Monáe must be recognized for her liminality. Like Badu, Monáe uses her music, videos, and personal style to exhibit the rele-vance of black futures to current and past conceptions of blackness. More-over, both artists draw upon multiple black histories in their work, connect-ing the black humanist search for authenticity and the black posthumanist embrace of fluidity.

Monáe's "Q.U.E.E.N." video takes place within a liminal setting, one si-multaneously historical, contemporary, and futuristic. As the opening cred-its roll, a voiceover begins, announcing the existence of the "Time Coun-cil," a future-located organization devoted to "stop[ping] rebels that time travel" (Monáe). The voice becomes digitally embodied: a monitor displays the speaking subject as a light-skinned, racially ambiguous woman who greets the two young, black women who enter the "PROJECT Q.U.E.E.N." exhibit at the Time Council's "Living Museum" (Monáe). The women—and more so the video's viewers—find themselves ensconced in multiple time periods. The women visit in the present a museum that showcases "legend-ary rebels," including two loincloth-wearing men and "Badoula Oblongata" (a pseudonym or persona adopted by Badu), as well as Monáe and several besuited members of her Wondaland Records roster, "frozen in suspended animation" (Monáe). Viewers experience even greater temporal liminality by observing a futuristic museum that displays as historical artifacts individu-als who might not yet exist in our present (for example, Badoula Oblongata can be considered a fantastical, futuristic version of Badu).

While multiple temporalities intertwine in the video, ideas about the future shape the historical and contemporary significance of the legendary rebels, including their promotion of black identities. Throughout the video for "Q.U.E.E.N.," understandings of the past and present intersect with expectations of what the future will bring, prompting viewers to call into question the received histories of black identity. When the two museum visi-tors play Monáe's record and thus reanimate those exhibited, viewers wit-ness the frozen rebels' movement in seemingly anachronistic situations. First, the black men in loincloths play an electric guitar and drum set. While the musicians' costuming and white body paint indicate their membership in an indigenous tribe, the men, who demonstrate their facility with contemporary and, at least in the case of the guitar, Western instruments, refuse to be located in a specific place or time. As opposed to the indigenous subjects of Jimmy Nelson's photography book *Before They Pass Away*, who, Elissa Washuta argues, stand as symbols of a static historical blackness, the tribesmen of "Q.U.E.E.N." mock viewers who might see them as purely historical or on the verge of extinction. The men, located in futuristic museum, embody posthuman liminality, offering the possibility that past and present understandings of indigenous identities may be derived from the future.

The video's promotion of temporal liminality continues with its depictions of Wondaland Records' artists. Monáe launched Wondaland Records in 2015—two years after the "Q.U.E.E.N." video premiered—signing many members of her former Atlanta-based artist collective, the Wondaland Arts Society. While watching the video, viewers may recognize Monáe, Jidenna, and other Wondaland artists as existing in the present, but the personas portrayed in "Q.U.E.E.N." visit from the past and the future. The voiceover at the beginning of the video announces that investigators "are still deciphering the nature of" Wondaland's weapons initiative program and "hunting the various freedom movements that Wondaland disguised as songs, emotion pictures, and works of art" (Monáe). The very mention of "Wondaland" in the voiceover conveys temporal liminality: today, "Wondaland" evokes Wondaland Records, but when the video came out in 2013, "Wondaland" likely referred to the Wondaland Arts Society (though other possibilities remain available, since the video features people with the ability to time travel). Although the Wondaland Arts Society no longer exists, its members' music, videos, and artwork can be found in the present; moreover, archives of the society's web page feature proclamations of temporal flexibility, with Wondaland music deemed "the weapon of the future" (Wondaland). Additionally, Monáe—the singer, genomic "mother" of the android Cindi Mayweather, and "notorious leader" of Wondaland—presents herself as a musical weapon from the future: the liner notes to her 2010 album *The ArchAndroid* proclaim that she time travels from the year 2719 (English and Kim 219).

In the "Q.U.E.E.N." video, Monáe's Wondaland artists promote the power of posthumanism not only through their presence but also, paradoxically, by interacting with objects from the past. When the museum's visitors play Monáe's record, two reanimated Wondaland men—Chuck Lightning and Nate Wonder, who make up the duo Deep Cotton—transport themselves from a glass display case by clapping their hands. Once free from the case, Lightning sits at a typewriter, repeatedly keying, "We will create and destroy ten art movements in ten years," while Wonder appears standing with a glowing incandescent light bulb in his hand (Monáe). At the typewriter, Lightning draws upon the viewer's expectations that the future will disrupt present and past ideas about history and identity. Lightning seems old fashioned when considered in the context of writers who utilize laptops and tablets. However, the message keyed—"We will create and destroy ten art movements in ten years"—resists historicization: Lightning presents the creation of history, the art movements referenced in the typing, in future tense ("We *will* create and destroy ten art movements in ten years" [emphasis mine]). The typing, and the video as a whole, support Eshun's claim that Afrofuturist history "arrives from the future" (*More* 00[–005]). Viewers can only imagine what the future will bring, what the art movements will look like, and why the Wondaland collective would want to destroy them.

The powers of the Wondaland members featured in the "Q.U.E.E.N." video appear future based, since the members possess knowledge denied to the viewer. The now-archived Wondaland Arts Society website states that its members enjoy the "new and ancient" force called "WISM," which brings together "Love. Sex. Wisdom. Magic and Wonder" (Wondaland). Additionally, the society proclaims a belief in Moore's Law, the conjecture that approximately every two years the processing capabilities of computers double (Wondaland). Together, these concepts show that Wondaland members develop their abilities and philosophies not only from the recognition of history (the "ancient" aspect of WISM and the repeating, historical pattern of Moore's law) but also their projections of the future (the "new" component of WISM and the predicted doubling of processing speeds).

Monáe's video depicts these liminal understandings of black identity and power during the scenes featuring Deep Cotton's Wonder holding the light bulb. The incandescent bulb looks archaic when compared to compact florescent or LED lights, and the use of past technologies is made stranger when the viewer remembers that Wonder visits from the future: certainly he enjoys more advanced technologies, yet he engages with equipment outdated in our present. However, the absence of a power source that would explain the bulb's glow indicates that Wonder accesses or produces an energy source not yet understood by the viewer, a source originating in the future.

This future-based power transforms Wonder from passive museum object to active time-traveling subject. If the viewer must imagine the future as a site of power for Wonder, then his identity, including his racial identity, might be understood to develop from the future as well.

With history removed as the ruling factor in determining blackness, the future becomes available as a site for the development of black power and identity. While music theorists and science fiction scholars have undertaken posthumanist and Afrofuturist readings for more than a decade, these theories have relevance for works in other genres, including those genres that seem resistant to futurist projections. Like Afrofuturist music and stories, works of contemporary historical fiction, including the neo–slave narrative *Corregidora*, participate in the posthumanist project of locating black power in the future as well as the present and past. In *Corregidora*, Jones's protagonist uses the liminality made possible by music first to reposition herself and her family in relation to their traumatic history and second to create a future for herself by becoming a different type of mother: the creator of a community.

AFROFUTURIST TEMPO-RALITY IN
GAYL JONES'S *CORREGIDORA*

In her 1975 novel, *Corregidora*, a text that spans from the late 1940s to the late 1960s but is peppered with stark descriptions of the physical, emotional, and sexual abuse a family of women suffered during slavery, Jones presents music as a tool through which her protagonist, Ursa Corregidora, initially reproduces but eventually alters her family's moribund history. Ursa sings the blues, a genre that, like Afrofuturist and jazz music, engages simultaneously with historical and futurist tropes. The blues allows Ursa to bring the histories of her enslaved ancestors into being through song and also create a new vision for the future that shapes her understanding of her past and present experiences. This two-part project results in inconclusive readings about Ursa's power at the conclusion of the novel: we do not know if Ursa repeats the past and reunites with her abusive ex-husband, though we are made aware that she refuses to reproduce one history and become, like her great-grandmother before her, a perpetrator of violence against the man who wronged her. However, the place of possibility in which Jones leaves her characters and readers emphasizes the power that can be drawn—

potentially, at least—from a liminal subjectivity. Recognizing Ursa's subjectivity as oriented toward the past, present, and future means that we cannot situate her—or her foremothers in the novel or black women and men from other works of historical fiction—as a fixture in or bearer of an unchanging history. Instead, we must acknowledge that posthuman liminality offers a constantly renewing source of agency for Ursa, her family, and her community.

Liminality becomes important early in the novel *Corregidora*. Ursa finds herself both estranged from and consumed by her family history in the present. While her mother, grandmother, and great-grandmother occupy her thoughts, Ursa struggles with her lack of a physical (specifically, uterine) connection to the women in her family. Following a domestic dispute with her first husband, Mutt, Ursa suffers a miscarriage and undergoes an emergency hysterectomy (*Corregidora* 15). Because of her inability to biologically continue her family line following the procedure, Ursa feels alienated from her foremothers, who stress the importance of keeping their history alive by producing children who will carry the stories of their ancestors' suffering into the future.

While Ursa possesses a liminal subjectivity, given her position both inside and outside the family line, her foremothers' narrative, passed on through the maternal body, reflects an engagement with a single, static history. Specifically, the family narrative relies on history to authenticate those experiences that have received no legal and insufficient cultural validation. Since the age of five, Ursa has heard stories from her foremothers about the necessity of communicating through the female body the horrors endured at the hands of the "Portuguese slave breeder and whoremonger" Simon Corregidora (*Corregidora* 8–9). Corregidora raped and impregnated Ursa's great-grandmother and grandmother (his own child), whom he owned as slaves. Because no written evidence of this abuse exists, Ursa's foremothers ask each female member of the family to contribute evidence by "*making generations*" (producing children) who will carry the stories of Corregidora's past offenses into the future (*Corregidora* 22). Ursa states: "My great-grandmama told my grandmama the part she lived through that my grandmama didn't live through and my grandmama told my mama what they both lived through and my mama told me what they all lived through and we were suppose to pass it down like that from generation to generation so we'd never forget" (*Corregidora* 9). Ursa's foremothers rely on a family-based oral tradition to validate their historical experiences. Their stories carry the past into the present and future as they give ongoing life to Corregidora and his crimes.

In addition to propagating the family narrative rhetorically, female children stand as biological artifacts of Corregidora's sexual abuses. "*I'm leaving evidence*," her great-grandmother says, speaking of the stories she has told and the family she has produced. "*And you got to leave evidence too. And your children got to leave evidence. And when it come time to hold up the evidence, we got to have evidence to hold up*" (*Corregidora* 14). Ursa's great-grandmother, grandmother, and mother offer their bodies and the bodies of their children as confirmation of Corregidora's past crimes. These women expect that Ursa will likewise perpetuate the family line and transform her body and the bodies of her offspring into the body of history or body of evidence to be presented against Corregidora on Judgment Day (*Corregidora* 41).

Through their procreative project, Ursa's foremothers participate in the obstruction of black subjectivity: they historicize the women of the family as well as the future of the family line. Certainly, the women of Jones's novel work to bring the past into the present and future. Making generations necessarily implies some type of forward movement. However, rather than attempting to rewrite or respond to history, as seen in other black humanistic efforts, the women of *Corregidora* carry forward a fixed history. Moreover, the women authenticate their present and future experiences by linking them to particular past events. Ursa's great-grandmother admits that the past continues to shape the women in their family, marking them as messengers of a history written by their oppressors: "*They burned all the documents, Ursa, but they didn't burn what they put in their minds. We got to burn out what they put in our minds, like you burn out a wound. Except we got to keep what we need to bear witness. That scar that's left to bear witness. We got to keep it as visible as our blood*" (*Corregidora* 72). Like the mark of race that, according to Hortense J. Spillers, historicizes the contemporary black subject, the scar that bears witness to Corregidora's crimes hinders Ursa as she works to develop a future distinct from her family history.[3]

The family's focus on an unchanging version of history represents a perversion of the black humanist agenda. While practitioners of black humanism may honor a debt to history that black posthumanist theorists avoid, the history embraced by black humanists must be understood as flexible and mutable. The focus on a fixed history in *Corregidora* situates Ursa's foremothers as devoted to a destructive form of humanism that limits the development and even the existence of the individual in the present and future. Ursa learns that in order to give her life and the lives of her foremothers purpose, she must exist as an historical object—a physical record of Corregidora's crimes—rather than as a present- or future-oriented subject. Like Corregidora himself, the women of Ursa's family objectify the female body, perpetuating its use in what Camille Passalacqua calls "a paradigm of production and power" (150). The expectation that Ursa will use her body to preserve and sustain history traps her in "a cycle of trauma": rather than freeing her family from the horrors of their history, the imperative that she tell their story through her body—her babies—makes her enslaved to the past (Passalacqua 146). Ursa's second husband, Tadpole, notes that the focus on "making generations" shared by the women of Ursa's family mirrors Corregidora's objectives: "Procreation. That could also be a slave-breeder's way of thinking" (*Corregidora* 22). Tadpole's comment points to the oppressive nature of the strategies for empowerment employed by Ursa's family. Situating the body as a repository for historical trauma means that the individual cannot escape this suffering.

Although Ursa cannot carry a child following her hysterectomy, the destiny assigned by her foremothers continues to control her. Reflecting on her music, Ursa realizes that she has been using her singing and songwriting abilities to give birth to the stories of Corregidora that her foremothers impregnated her with, which brings her family history into the present. Ursa states, "*They* [her foremothers] *squeezed Corregidora into me, and I sung back in return. I would have rather sung her memory* [stories of her mother's life unrelated to tales of Corregidora] *if I'd had to sing any. What about my own?*" (*Corregidora* 103). Ursa understands that her perception of herself has been stifled by what Sirène Harb calls "stagnant versions of history and identity" (118). As she comes to realize that her much-discussed family history threatens to consume her, Ursa repudiates her ancestors' strategies for fighting oppression and commits to changing her blues.

The liminality of blues music allows Ursa to alter her family history and personal identity. Blues music draws from historical forms (such as call-and-response form) but allows for the expression of individuality through the future-focused action of improvisation. Houston A. Baker notes that the "instrumental rhythms" of the blues "suggest change, movement, action, continuance, unlimited and unending possibility" (8). While Baker's emphasis on change and continuance reveals that the blues relies on the past as a reference point, the terms also indicate the instability of history, since the futurist elements of the blues keep its historical components in a state of flux. In its creation of the new and "rememory" of the bygone and extant (Morrison, Beloved 36), the blues engages with early iterations of Iton's "black fantastic," the "notions of being that are inevitably aligned with, in conversation with, against, and articulated beyond the boundaries of the modern" (16). By exceeding the modern—which marks the black subject as less-than-human—and entering the fantastic, the blues anticipates Afrofuturism's embrace of ideological, temporal, and subjective boundary crossings.

We can see the fluidity of boundaries in one of the hallmarks of the blues form, the "blue note." The blue note is "a musical note expressed with a slight deviation"—specifically, a drop in pitch—"from its standard temperament" (P. Jones 166). Grandt situates the blue note as existing in a "crossroads," a place "neither here nor there, defying the fixity of space and text, and yet a vital aspect of the story being told" (Shaping 80). In terms of temporality, the blue note brings together the past (the standard temperament, the security of what has come before) and the future (the slight derivation from the historical precedent, the excitement of what is new).

Carlyle Van Thompson argues that the blue note and other elements of the blues form appear in Jones's text via Ursa's repeating but varied statements about each of her foremothers sharing "the part [of family's abuse] she lived through" (Thompson 75–76; Corregidora 9). Moreover, the blue note's liminality ties to Ursa's motivation for making music. Her blues reflects her dedication both to continuing her foremothers' historical project (her acknowledgment of the "standard temperament") and to modifying the method through which she brings their past into the present and future (her "slight deviation" from the established pattern).

Jones further draws upon the blues tradition's liminality with her use of the break, a space of transition from one moment to the next. Albert Murray writes that the blues break is "a very special kind of ad-lib bridge passage or cadenzalike interlude between two musical phrases that are separated by an interruption or interval in the established cadence" (99). Murray compares the function of the break passage in blues with the function of a colon in a sentence: the break, like a colon, signals a pause in the "established flow of the rhythm and the melody" but not a full stop (99). During the break, a musician improvises, playing about four bars solo, before the ensemble falls back in and the rhythm and melody are restored (Murray 99). When considered in terms of temporality, the break can be understood to join the music of the past and the music of the future, given that the solo played during the break disrupts yet also dissolves into the established musical form.

Blues breaks appear throughout *Corregidora*, often signaled by Jones's use of broken prose passages and italicized text. Donia Elizabeth Allen asserts that the breaks draw attention to places in the novel where "boundaries are confused" and "characters are unable to distinguish where they end and the memories and stories their ancestors passed on to them begin" (266). While, as Allen illustrates, break passages in the novel indicate moments of internal or external chaos, the breaks also function as spaces in which Ursa moves among temporalities and, significantly, engages with the future.

During one such break, an imagined narration tracing her development from child to adult, Ursa asserts, "*I am Ursa Corregidora. I have tears for eyes. I was made to touch my past at an early age. I found it on my mother's tiddies. In her milk. Let no one pollute my music. I will dig out their temples. I will pluck out their eyes*" (*Corregidora* 77). Ursa's proclamation of her identity during the break begins with her return to the position of a child, the time when she was first confronted with stories of Corregidora, but moves into a future time when she will fight those who would attempt to pollute her music, when she will resist her foremothers' demand that she bear and birth only the stories of their past pains. Ursa's turn toward the future gains additional significance when considering the context in which the break passage occurs: she makes her statement of identity during a dream in which she talks to Corregidora and her great grandmother, two figures from the past who infringe upon her present and future. Thus, while the break denotes, according to Allen, the difficulty Ursa faces in "setting boundaries of all kinds, physical, emotional, between past and present," the break also marks a moment where she recognizes "the importance of coming to voice, of being able to distinguish the voices of one's ancestors and one's own" (272). As such, the break functions as a liminal space where past, present, and future temporalities and self and other identities overlap and intersect. In this liminal space, Ursa acknowledges the power of history—for example, her pronouncement that she has "tears for eyes" indicates that her foremothers' past continues to shape her present existence—but she also shows that the history of the Corregidora women has changed by asserting her independence from her foremothers' predictions for the future.

The presence of the liminal blues form in *Corregidora* necessitates an exploration of the novel's multiple temporalities. As Madhu Dubey argues, the plot of Jones's novel "raises the possibility that an uncritical preoccupation with the mother's past might obstruct rather than assist the development of the daughter's story" (253). In addition to recognizing the fixation on the past within the novel, we must resist "an uncritical preoccupation" with history in our readings of the text. Scholars such as Missy Dehn Kubitschek and Ashraf H. A. Rushdy offer productive humanist readings of Jones's novel, asserting that Ursa's subjectivity develops from her ability to rewrite the past (Kubitschek 147; Rushdy, *Remembering* 55). Jones likewise suggests the applicability of historical, humanist interpretations of texts. She asserts, "To liberate their voices from the often tyrannic frame of another's outlook, many world literatures continue to look to their own folklores and oral modes for forms, themes, tastes, conceptions of symmetry, time, space, detail, and human values" (*Liberating* 192). Jones's assessment of tradition-focused strategies for communicating applies to *Corregidora*, since her protagonist seeks to liberate her voice through the African American genre of the blues.

Discovering an empowered black identity through a link to history is not problematic; however, finding that empowerment must be derived solely from a tie to history minimizes the potential of present and future conceptions of blackness, as Jones's characters demonstrate. Accordingly, in *Corregidora*, Ursa's blues conveys the role the present and future play in shaping subjectivity and history. In an interview with Michael S. Harper about her use of the blues in her fiction, Jones suggests that the blues has power because of its ability to bring several emotions together. She asserts, "Blues talks about the simultaneity of good and bad, as feeling, as something felt. [. . .] Blues acknowledges all different kinds of feelings at once" (Jones and Harper 700). Later, in *Liberating Voices*, her analysis of the oral tradition in black literature, Jones brings the concept of time into her assessment of the genre's take on emotion, noting, "Blues pulls together and asserts identity (self and other) through clarification and playing back of experiences and meanings" (93). Jones's statements about the blues convey that time periods intertwine and overlap within the genre: futures exist in the present, as do pasts. Accordingly, a critical examination of the blues—like a critical examination of black humanism and black posthumanism—requires an engagement with multiple, complex pasts, presents, and futures.

In *Corregidora*, reading for temporal liminality highlights moments when

Ursa draws power not only from the past but also from the future. For instance, Ursa states that when writing her music, she strives to compose a song that brings the future and past together: "I wanted a song that would touch me, touch my life and theirs. A Portuguese song, but not a Portuguese song. A new world song. A song branded in the new world" (Corregidora 59). Ursa's differentiation between "my life and theirs" and a "Portuguese song" and "not a Portuguese song" signals that she separates herself from the oppressive history of her family. While she desires to join her foremothers' stories with her own, she views her music as a tool she can use to build and protect a future distinct from her family's past. Moreover, the novel reveals that Ursa's future vision for her music influences her understanding of the family's narrative: the future she imagines can "touch" or shape her foremothers' history. Rushdy joins Keith Byerman in arguing that Ursa's singing of the blues signals that Jones's character has "found a way to translate into a cultural artifact the oppressive history of the Corregidora women" (Rushdy, Remembering 42; Byerman, "Fingering" 178), a type of creation that changes her relationship with her family's history and also changes the history itself. Unlike her great-grandmother, grandmother, and mother, who seek to bring their fixed history into the present and future, Ursa uses her vision for the future to revise the family legacy.

Ursa draws a distinction between interconnected temporalities, which she allows, and determinant histories, which she rejects. As such, Ursa's blues reflects the power of posthuman liminality. Indeed, Eshun insists that Afrofuturist music "is all in the breaks," the gaps between listening to specific artists and tracks and reevaluating "what you took to be the limits of Black Music" and "what you took Black Music to be" (More oo[–oo2]). While he does not mention the blues specifically, Eshun's focus on the break suggests that the blues break can function as a liminal space. Through her blues, Ursa harnesses the power of liminality, rewriting the story of her family's historical suffering and extending their family line in new ways. She rejects her foremothers' command to give birth to generations in order to perpetuate an unchanged history, yet her songs create a community. Her friends and co-workers note that after her hysterectomy, Ursa's voice develops a tone or quality that draws the listener in: "You got a hard kind of voice," her boss Max states. "You know, like callused hands. Strong and hard but gentle underneath. Strong but gentle too. The kind of voice that can hurt you. I can't explain it. Hurt you and make you still want to listen"

(*Corregidora* 96). Both Tadpole and Ursa's friend Cat explain that the audience is attracted to Ursa's ability to communicate her suffering, which indicates that Ursa does accomplish her foremothers' goal of bringing an historical pain into the present. Tad tells Ursa that when she was singing, her voice "sounded like it had sweat in it. Like you were pulling everything out of yourself. You were beautiful, sweet" (*Corregidora* 54). Cat similarly states, "Your voice sounds a little strained, that's all. But if I hadn't heard you before, I wouldn't notice anything. I'd still be moved. Maybe even moved more, because it sounds like you been through something. Before it was beautiful too, but you sound like you been through more now" (*Corregidora* 44).

As her listeners' words intimate, Ursa brings the trauma of the past—her foremothers' and her own—together with her hope for the future. While she resists her foremothers' singular focus on history, she does not ignore history itself—since she's embraced a liminal identity, she could not even if she wanted to. However, the end of Jones's novel signals that Ursa has begun to see her story as fluid, as beholden to the future as much as the past. "I have to make my own kind of life," Ursa tells her mother. "I have to make some kind of life for myself" (*Corregidora* 111). When her mother asks, "Corregidora's never been enough for you, has it?", she, like Jones's reader, already knows that Ursa's answer will be no (*Corregidora* 111). In addition to directly rejecting her foremothers' value system, Ursa's statement about building a future—her assertion that she has "to make some kind of life" for herself—contrasts with her mother's rhetorical link between her daughter's past and present. When Ursa's mother states, "Corregidora's never been enough for you," she uses the contracted phrase "has never been" to join Ursa's childhood feelings and current outlook on the Corregidora family legacy. The distinction between Ursa's present- and future-focused comments and her mother's past- and present-concerned question marks Ursa's break from her foremothers' humanist project.

By using her blues to construct an alternative history and future, Ursa becomes a new type of mother: the creator and nurturer of a community. Ursa does not simply change the manner through which she completes the tasks set out for her by her foremothers; instead, she uses her music to separate herself from their ongoing and unchanging past. Rather than allowing her body to be sacrificed as the bodies of her foremothers were, Ursa uses her voice to free them and herself from the oppression Corregidora initiated and the women in her family perpetuated. Like the singing women at the conclusion of Toni Morrison's *Beloved* whose wordless songs pour from their bodies and communicate a suffering larger than them, Ursa shares her story and the stories of her ancestors through her music. Her singing of the blues draws the community into the family's tale, making not one person— a child—responsible for their history but asking for all of the community to participate in the creation of counternarratives. In widening and broadening her family line through the blues, Ursa allows others to bear the burden of keeping her family history alive, which gives her room to create a future for herself and to revise the legacy of the Corregidora women. This revision of her family legacy—the move to use her musical vision for the future to transform her understanding of the past—positions Ursa's blues as a liminal genre.

In bringing together multiple temporalities and privileging the potential of the future, Jones's novel demonstrates the power of posthumanism. Significantly, *Corregidora* features an open, ambiguous ending: readers are unsure of how Ursa's relationship with her ex-husband, Mutt, will develop. While Ursa considers reliving with Mutt the violent assault she has been told her great-grandmother enacted against Corregidora before escaping his enslavement, she decides not to recreate this past (Rushdy, *Remembering* 48, 53–54). Instead, she enters an unknown future. The place of possibility in which Jones leaves her characters and readers emphasizes the power that can be drawn from a future-focused subjectivity. As Eshun states, "The future is a much better guide to the present than the past" (*More* oo[–ooı]). Accordingly, readers should not assume that Ursa's life will be a repetition of her foremothers' history: we do not know what will happen. Forging links across time, space, and personhood propels the black subject into a visionary position where all acts, including those that may seem preordained, can be altered. By creating new spaces and places for fuller black expression, Jones, like Badu and Monáe, promotes both alternative black histories and potential black futures. The relationship between liminal temporalities and subjectivities reveals itself in Afrofuturist music and historical fiction as well as other genres, including visual art, speculative fiction, and film.

CHAPTER 4

Posthuman Multiple Consciousness in Octavia E. Butler's Science Fiction

In 2016, ten years after her death, Octavia E. Butler experienced a rebirth. Arguably, Butler, the best-known black woman science fiction writer, never disappeared: the Carl Brandon Society established in 2006 the Octavia E. Butler Memorial Scholarship to support writers of color at the Clarion and Clarion West workshops; Conseula Francis collected Butler's interviews in *Conversations with Octavia Butler* in 2009; and the e-book *Unexpected Stories*, which makes available the previously unpublished "A Necessary Being" and "Childfinder," appeared in 2014. Additionally, two separate books of science fiction inspired by Butler materialized after her passing: *Near Kin: A Collection of Words and Art Inspired by Octavia Estelle Butler* (Lecrivain 2014) and *Octavia's Brood: Science Fiction from Social Movements* (Imarisha and brown 2015).

Yet 2016 stands as an important year for Butler as well as for the writers and scholars inspired by her. In addition to the Octavia E. Butler Literary Society holding the first Butler-dedicated conference that February, the Los Angeles arts organization Clockshop—in conjunction with the Huntington and other cultural institutions—organized *Radio Imagination*, a yearlong celebration of everything Butler. *Radio Imagination* featured a Butler-themed contemporary art exhibition that ran from October 1, 2016, through January 7, 2017. Additionally, the project supported musicians, poets, and creative nonfiction writers in the production of their work and hosted legacy tours, film screenings, panel discussions, and readings (Clockshop). With dozens of contemporary artists, writers, and scholars bringing Butler-inspired texts into being, *Radio Imagination* and other Butler-centric productions continue to make Butler's presence felt, allowing her to transcend time and space.

Transcendence and transformation additionally mark Butler's oeuvre. Her science fiction deals with boundary crossings that inspire new—and often traumatic—forms of being. In several of her works, Butler uses historical imagery of the Middle Passage to convey physical as well as metaphysical shifts that extend beyond the past and into the present and future. In *Wild Seed* (1980), Anyanwu, an immortal shape shifter, makes the journey from Africa to colonial America in the company of Doro, an immortal body snatcher. While Anyanwu escapes slavery in Benin and becomes a reluctant slaver in what is now Nigeria, her Middle Passage experience with Doro marks her shift from subject to object. Like her kin on the ship and, later, the shore, Anyanwu faces Doro's beatings, manipulations, and rapes. During their centuries together, Doro tells her, "You'll only be in danger if you disobey me" and "Anyanwu, you must not leave me!" (Butler, *Wild* 271, 294), positioning Anyanwu as an object necessary for sustaining his humanity and agency. Although Anyanwu escapes Doro's authority by turning herself into an animal, when she returns to human form she finds herself ruled by him much in the same way white slave traders and owners dominate her dark-skinned descendants.

Anyanwu's Middle Passage experience—her travel from Africa to colonial New York aboard a slave ship—transforms the shape shifter. While Anyanwu can alter her body from female to male, young to old, and human to animal, the Middle Passage journey signals her conversion from self-possessed subject to Doro-directed object. The subject–object transition that occurs for the fictional Anyanwu mirrors that of historical captured Africans during the Middle Passage. Toni Morrison, Greg Tate, Calvin L. Warren, and Kodwo Eshun argue that the Middle Passage stands as the moment in history when black subjects became abstracted into metaphysical elements or objects (Gilroy, *Small* 178; Eshun, "Further" 297–98; Warren 237).[1] As Warren asserts, "the literal destruction of black bodies" during and following the transatlantic slave voyage enables "the psychic, economic, and philosophical resources for modernity to objectify, forget, and ultimately obliterate Being" (237). With the Middle Passage standing in for the bar that, according to Tate, separates signifier from signified, the black body becomes "objectified, infused with exchange value, and rendered malleable within a sociopolitical order" of white power (Eshun, "Further" 297–98; Warren 226, 237).

In order to recognize and overcome the abstraction of black bodies and identities that began with the Middle Passage, new types of consciousness must be developed. If W. E. B. Du Bois's double consciousness describes the ability to recognize the black body's signification in white culture, and

Frantz Fanon's triple consciousness marks an awareness of the move from black subject to black object within this system, then the multiple consciousness of black posthumanism and Afrofuturism assists the black individual in viewing the self from outside the system of signification altogether. Eshun asserts that the "triple consciousness, quadruple consciousness" of Afrofuturism makes the black subject privy to "previously inaccessible alienations" ("Further" 298). Eshun's "previously inaccessible alienations" correspond to the abstraction of blackness since the Middle Passage, the positioning of the sign of blackness within the ontology and cosmology of white power. Like Afrofuturism's triple or quadruple consciousness, black posthumanism's *multiple consciousness* allows the subject to understand and potentially surmount this alienation. Viewing identity as part of but separate from the system of signification corresponds with the posthuman imperative to blur dividing lines but celebrate distinctions between temporalities and subjectivities, an imperative reflected in posthuman constructions of identity and solidarity.

Transformative Middle Passage experiences in Butler's science fiction cultivate a posthuman multiple consciousness that allows characters and readers to recognize blackness both within and outside of the ontology and cosmology of white power. As Nadine Flagel argues, "Much speculative fiction is explicitly or implicitly engaged with issues of slavery and freedom, possession and liberation, but divorces these issues from the material conditions of slavery" (224). While Butler features literal and metaphorical Middle Passages in several of her works, including *Wild Seed* (as mentioned above), *Dawn* (1987), and "Bloodchild" (1984), in the novel *Kindred* (1979) Butler directly acknowledges the material conditions of slavery that, as Flagel points out, speculative and science fiction authors all-too-often ignore. Butler's use of time travel in the neo–slave narrative *Kindred* compels her African American protagonist, Dana Franklin, to undergo alienating notions of racial identity in the past, present, and future. Dana's Middle Passage experiences aid her development of a posthuman multiple consciousness through which she recognizes both temporality and subjectivity as liminal. Although Warren and Eshun argue that black subjectivity exists only in the past—prior to the Middle Passage—and Warren warns that the achievement of black subjectivity in the future would mean the end of blackness as we know it (Eshun, "Further" 298; Warren 244), Dana, as a possessor of posthuman multiple consciousness, resides within a liminal temporality and, as such, understands that black subjectivity exists in those places accepted as well as those denied: the past, present, and future.

Additionally, Butler's posthumously published "A Necessary Being" (2014) models posthuman multiple consciousness for readers who may otherwise struggle to view any racial identity as distinct from white supremacy. By depicting power relations in a world unlike ours, Butler enables her readers to understand races and cultures as connected to but differentiated from one another. Specifically, in "A Necessary Being" Butler presents readers with the familiar concept of hierarchies based on skin color, yet through her character development, she dismisses the subsumption of one race under another. Butler's otherworldly protagonist, a blue-fleshed female named Tahneh, sees herself as part of and also distinct from the Kohn culture in which she exists, paradoxically, as both ruler and slave. By considering power systems in this alien environment—an environment distinct from white, Western cosmologies—readers can join Tahneh in cultivating a posthuman multiple consciousness and acknowledging new ways of understanding both self and other identities.

DOUBLE AND TRIPLE CONSCIOUSNESS

The Middle Passage commences a series of psychological, physical, and ontological shifts for captured Africans. Aboard ships and on soil, women, men, and children experience a violence that literally and figuratively disrupts black subjectivity. Valérie Loichot asserts, "The slave family is marked by a series of amputations: an immense and abrupt severing from original African roots and memory; a dismemberment of family units by practices of kidnapping or selling; literal amputations of limbs of fugitive slaves; splits between bodies turned into economic tools of production and mind; substitution of mothering and fathering by breeding; and attempted disassociation of humanity from black subjects" (41). The Middle Passage alters not only black communities and bodies in the past but also black identities in the present. The effects of enslavement on the form and concept of blackness—as Loichot says, the relationship between black subjectivity and humanity—means that the Middle Passage shapes historical and contemporary ideas of race.

Theorizing the Middle Passage extends the transatlantic slave trade beyond the four centuries of trauma that triangulated Africa, Europe, and

the Americas. For instance, Morrison finds that Middle Passage dislocations foreshadow modernist alienations (Gilroy, *Small* 178). Tate extends
these Middle Passage dislocations to the field of semiotics, arguing that the
Middle Passage operates as the bar between signifier and signified (Eshun,
"Further" 297–98). Warren furthers Tate's semiotic approach, asserting
that the meaninglessness of signification following the Middle Passage in-
stitutes a black nihilism. And Eshun "reroutes" the alien abductions of the
Middle Passage through contemporary Afrofuturist science fictions in order to offer alternative histories and futures ("Further" 300). Each of these
theorists marks the Middle Passage as both a defining, centuries-long moment in history as well as an experience that exceeds the specific time period
during which it occurs. Moreover, each theorist recognizes that during and
following the Middle Passage, constructions of blackness develop in opposition to, yet support of, whiteness.

Theories of black identity provide concrete examples of the paradoxical
opposition to and support of white power structures cultivated by constructions of blackness since the Middle Passage. Du Bois's double consciousness
describes the internalization of both black- and white-determined ideas of
blackness. He explains that the black subject inhabits "a world which yields
him no true self-consciousness, but only lets him see himself through the
revelation of the other world" (Du Bois 38). The "other world"—the white
world—views the black subject with "amused contempt and pity," which Du
Bois argues compels the black subject to observe himself similarly (38). Du
Bois's black subject, though situated in opposition to the "other world" of
the white subject, supports white power structures with his "longing to attain self-conscious manhood, to merge his double self into a better and truer
self" (39)—a self determined by or at least incorporating white-authored
notions of humanity.

Du Bois describes a system of signification in which whiteness shapes
the cultural significance of blackness. Although his assertion of a double
consciousness suggests the existence of a "Negro" consciousness distinct
from a white "American" consciousness (Du Bois 38), white supremacy
shapes both entities. Rejecting the mutual exclusivity of blackness and
whiteness in Du Boisian double consciousness, Paul Gilroy argues that Du
Bois's theory acknowledges the "transformation and fragmentation of the
integral racial self," indicating that although ideas of blackness vary across
black communities, "constricting or absolutist understandings of ethnic-

ity" driven by white power structures limit the expression of black humanity (Black 138). As Gilroy asserts, Du Bois's "two warring ideals" have "democratic potential disfigured by white supremacy" (Du Bois 38; Gilroy, Black 113); in other words, whiteness, by cultivating meaning through the opposition of blackness, distorts blackness for blacks and whites.

Fanon similarly addresses the supremacy of white power structures in shaping ideas about blackness. However, whereas Du Bois posits a double consciousness, Fanon contends that blacks possess a "triple" personhood or consciousness. Like Du Bois, Fanon argues that the black individual exists as a subject and also in relation to the white other. Fanon then adds a third element: via the relation to the white other, the black individual loses subjectivity and occupies object status (84). Fanon expresses his desire to "be a man among other men," but he concludes that he has "made [himself] an object"—the third aspect of his triple consciousness—because "his inferiority comes into being through the other" (85, 83). Fanon's triple consciousness thus offers blacks not only a vision of black and white notions of blackness, as Du Bois's double consciousness does, but also a glimpse of the "other," the larger white power structure that shapes rhetorical concepts of race.

Despite labeling white supremacist systems as "other," neither Du Bois nor Fanon argues that blackness influences whiteness in the same way whiteness distorts blackness. Rejecting the equal reflexivity of blackness and whiteness, Fanon assigns triple consciousness specifically to black men and women:

> Ontology—once it is finally admitted as leaving existence by the wayside—does not permit us to understand the being of the black man. For not only must the black man be black; he must be black in relation to the white man. Some critics will take it on themselves to remind us that this proposition has a converse. I say that this is false. The black man has no ontological resistance in the eyes of the white man. Overnight the Negro has been given two frames of reference within which he has had to place himself. His metaphysics, or, less pretentiously, his customs and the sources on which they were based, were wiped out because they were in conflict with a civilization that did not know and that imposed itself on him. (82–83)

Diana Fuss explains that for Fanon, whiteness operates as a "transcendental signifier," a "self-identical, self-reproducing term" that proclaims freedom from blackness as well as "the very category of 'race'" (22). Fuss follows Fanon in asserting that whiteness, in mandating independence from racial categories, colonizes blackness and reserves subjectivity for whites alone (Fuss 23).

If white power structures regulate the rhetoric of race and the assignation of subjectivity, then blackness—even in its opposition to whiteness—supports white supremacy. Semiotics—what Warren calls the "very structure of meaning in the modern world"—depends upon the existence of blackness and, specifically, the othering of blackness, which takes the concrete form of "anti-black violence" during and following the Middle Passage (226). While Du Bois and Fanon explain through their theories of double and triple consciousness that antiblack violence exists as a byproduct of white supremacist systems, Warren positions black suffering as foundational to semiotics and Western metaphysics (237–38): "If literal black bodies sustain modernity and metaphysics—though various forms of captivity, terror, and subjection," he asks, "then what would emancipation entail for blacks? How do we allow metaphysics to self-consume and weaken when blackness nourishes metaphysics?" (Warren 239). Warren follows Morrison in interweaving the origins of modernity and black oppression, though he extends her premise by arguing that historical and contemporary American culture depends on antiblack violence.

Warren's black nihilist philosophy provides no answer to the problem of black suffering within white power structures; however, his argument that blackness contributes to the perpetuation of these structures indicates the need for a new type of consciousness: one that not only recognizes the impact of whiteness on black subjectivity (like Du Bois's double consciousness) and black metaphysics (like Fanon's triple consciousness) but also acknowledges the reflexive relationship of blackness and whiteness within white supremacist systems. Posthuman multiple consciousness affords this perspective. Posthuman multiple consciousness perceives black identities as contributing to but also potentially independent of white, Western metaphysics. In particular, considering identity within the temporal liminality of posthumanism allows the black subject to conceive of a future in which blackness destroys rather than facilitates black objectification. While Warren argues that this type of "'blackened' world" would put an "end to metaphysics" and "the world itself" (244), posthumanism projects non-apocalyptic possibilities for the future as well as the past and present.

MULTIPLE CONSCIOUSNESS AND BLACK
NIHILISM IN BUTLER'S *Kindred*

When read through the lens of posthuman multiple consciousness, black science fiction—including Afrofuturist texts concerning the oppression of black identities and objectification of black bodies in the past, present, or future—promotes the existence of black subjectivity throughout time. Eshun asserts that Afrofuturism relies on "extraterrestriality as a hyperbolic trope to explore the historical terms, the everyday implications of forcibly imposed dislocation, and the constitution of Black Atlantic subjectivities: from slave to negro to coloured to *evolué* to black to African to African American" ("Further" 298–99). Black science fiction's alien abductions mirror the black subject's real-world alienations in historical and contemporary white power structures. However, in addition to engaging with the past and present, black science fiction texts blend these time periods with the future to create a liminal temporality. By disrupting "the linear time of progress" and "the temporal logics that condemned black subjects to prehistory"—the time before the Middle Passage and slavery—black science fiction presents "a series of powerful competing futures that infiltrate the present at different rates" (Eshun, "Further" 297). Reading black science fiction through posthuman multiple consciousness shows that although the Middle Passage strips captured Africans of subjectivity, as Tate, Warren, and Eshun assert, the texts' liminal temporality brings black subjectivity into the present and future.

In her science fictional neo–slave narrative *Kindred*, Butler makes posthuman liminality literal through the depiction of time travel. Middle Passage experiences take Butler's characters not across the ocean but through time and space. Dana, Butler's African American protagonist, journeys between 1976 California, her present, and antebellum Maryland, her ancestral past. Even Dana's first trip back to 1811 or 1812 engages with the temporal, spatial, and subjective shifts indicative of the Middle Passage experience. On June 9, 1976—her twenty-sixth birthday—Dana feels "dizzy, nauseated" while organizing books in her new home with her husband, Kevin (Butler, *Kindred* 13). Dana's books, house, and husband "blur" into nonexistence as trees, a river, and a drowning child come into view (*Kindred* 13). Present changes to past, indoors to outdoors, and friend to foe—though Dana does not yet understand her fraught relationship with the white child, Rufus—during her voyage from 1976 to the 1810s. While these shifts seem like the direct exchange of opposites, Butler blurs not only Dana's vision but also the binaries. For instance, Dana draws upon her knowledge of artificial respiration from the present (or the future, considering the perspective of antebellum Dana) to save the child in the past (or the present, again keeping in mind Dana's antebellum point of view). Accordingly, seemingly distinct periods and places overlap for Dana not only during her Middle Passage travels between present and past but also during her time in each temporality.

Kindred's liminality allows both Butler's protagonist and her readers to consider race, and, in particular, blackness, within and outside of specific cosmologies of white power. The novel depicts the implications of Dana's blackness during both her personal present and her familial past. As a black woman in 1976, Dana faces racial bigotry and sexual harassment. Her co-worker murmurs, "Chocolate and vanilla porn!" when seeing her with Kevin, who is white, and Kevin's sister and brother-in-law as well as Dana's uncle object to the news of their interracial relationship (Kindred 56, 110). Although the novel suggests that Dana and Kevin have a happy and healthy marriage, 1970s gender roles relegate Dana to a subordinate position: both Dana and Kevin identify as writers, but Kevin, the "primary breadwinner" (Parham 1322), asks Dana to type his manuscripts. Similarly, Dana notes that after moving into their new house, Kevin leaves her to finish unpacking, since he "had stopped when he got his office in order" (Kindred 12). In both situations, Kevin changes his behavior after he recognizes Dana's discomfort, but Dana, and not Kevin, seeks reconciliation after their fights, and she makes excuses for Kevin's behavior. For example, Dana thinks that the "look" Kevin gives her in response to a passive-aggressive comment is not "as malevolent as it seem[s]" and that he would try "to intimidate [. . .] [s]trangers" but not her (Kindred 13). Considering these power imbalances, Marc Steinberg argues that Dana and Kevin's relationship "smacks of a kind of servitude," and the "line between slavery and marriage" becomes "blurred" as the novel continues (469). As Dana finds herself beholden to others—including her husband—both in the present and past, the influence of white power structures on black subjectivity becomes apparent to readers.

Late-twentieth-century conventions of race and gender intersect with early nineteenth-century customs when Kevin follows Dana through time to the antebellum Upper South. After Rufus meets Kevin and asks the white man, "Does Dana belong to you now?" Kevin affirms the boy's suspicion: "In a way," he answers. "She's my wife" (Kindred 60). The intolerance Dana and Kevin experience as an interracial couple in 1976 likewise returns, anachronistically speaking, in 1819, with Rufus, first, denying the plausibility of their relationship and, second, asserting its illegality. Rufus again conveys the period's white supremacist and patriarchal views when, near the end of the novel, he asks Dana to take the place of Alice—his unwilling wife and Dana's great-great-grandmother—as his lover. Lisa Yaszek notes, "The bargain seems perfectly reasonable to Rufus—after all, Dana and Alice are nearly identical doubles of one another, and black women are supposed to accede to the wishes of white men" ("Grim" 1063). Dana's performance as a slave during her time in Maryland exposes her to the physical and emotional violence born of black women's object status.

While Dana's position as a black woman within a white power structure shifts as she moves throughout time, her objectification persists. Steinberg asserts that Butler "assumes a non-Western conceptualization of history—one in which history is cyclical, not linear—in order to demonstrate ways in which certain forms of race and gender oppression continue late into the twentieth century and beyond" (467). Steinberg's argument about racism, when broadened to considerations of race in general, reveals that the temporal liminality in Kindred incorporates a subjective liminality: blackness—in relation to and distinct from whiteness and, in particular, white supremacy—holds historical as well as trans-temporal significance. Although Warren argues that the fantasy of political progress, represented by a linear timeline extending into the future of improved race relations, "allows one to disregard the historicity of anti-blackness and its continued legacy" (221), Butler's novel uses liminality rather than linearity to acknowledge white supremacy in the past, present, and future.

Specifically, Dana's temporal and subjective liminality imbue her with a posthuman multiple consciousness through which she situates blackness within and outside of white power structures. During her second peregrination between past and present, Dana meets a white patroller who attempts to rape her. Dana's fear propels her forward—or back—to the future, where she finds herself "kicking" and "clawing" Kevin, whom she mistakes for the patroller (Kindred 43). Kevin never physically threatens Dana in the novel, but his whiteness—when considered from her new, temporally liminal perspective—endangers her. Lauren J. Lacey asserts, "Dana has had to become a different kind of subject in order to see herself through the eyes of a white male patroller in the past, and the transition to the present is not particularly simple. Kevin's status as a white male is newly complicated for Dana by her experiences in the past" (75). In discussing Dana observing herself "through the eyes of a white male patroller," Lacey acknowledges Dana's multiple consciousness: Dana believes herself to be a subject, but when considering that the patroller views her as a body to be used, exchangeable for any of the other black female bodies she's "just like" (Kindred 42), she understands her object status. Loichot similarly acknowledges Dana's awareness of her object position, noting that "Dana realizes two important things at once. Her own name and body disappear under the function of the female slave, sexualized object at the mercy of the white master" (44). Dana's knowledge of her subordinate status in the past shapes her view of herself and others in the present when she attacks her husband upon her return to California. She positions blackness within the ontology of whiteness in the past as well as the present when she brings the historicity of her object status into her life with her husband.

However, posthuman multiple consciousness not only positions blackness within the ontology of whiteness but also provides a view of blackness divorced from white supremacy. Dana's subjectivity, when considered within the Middle Passage timeline suggested by Tate, Warren, and Eshun, shifts throughout Kindred. Specifically, time travel allows her to simultaneously possess and be denied the subjectivity of Middle Passage prehistory. If, as Eshun argues, black subjectivity exists only in "prehistory"—before the Middle Passage—then the existence of time travel in Kindred means that Dana can neither claim nor be denied subjectivity at any point in the story: her prehistory, like her present and future, is ubiquitous (Eshun, "Further" 297). According to Lacey, temporal liminality in the novel shapes Dana's understanding of herself: "Butler uses the device of time travel to create a narrative that absolutely refuses to see past and present as discrete, closed off, or even formal categories. Dana's life—her home, her life with her husband—are caught up in the demand to see the relationship between past and present as mutually constitutive. Throughout the novel, Butler emphasizes how difficult it is for Dana to 'leave the past behind'" (73). Indeed, Dana cannot "leave the past behind" because she always already inhabits the past: each Middle Passage venture takes Dana to a tripartite temporality. After her initial trip to the antebellum Upper South, Dana's travels to Maryland place her in a future-past—a past more recent than that of her previous visit—which becomes her present. Similarly, Dana's return to the "normalcy" of 1976 California situates her in a future-present—a present more recent than the one she left—which, considering the physical and emotional toll time travel exacts upon her, becomes part of her past. While the historical Middle Passage takes place during Dana's ancestral past, her personal Middle Passage experiences occur in the past, present, and future; accordingly, her "prehistory," her pre–Middle Passage subjectivity, simultaneously occurs within and exceeds all three temporalities.

However, *Kindred*'s temporal liminality means that Dana's post–Middle Passage objectification simultaneously occurs within and exceeds past, present, and future. If, as Tate argues, the Middle Passage marks the moment of the black subject's abstraction and objectification—that is, "the bar between signifier and the signified could be understood as standing for the Middle Passage that separated *signification* (meaning) from *sign* (letter)" (Eshun, "Further" 297)—then the final chapter of Butler's novel gives the bar physical and spatial significance. During her last trip to the past, Dana stabs Rufus to prevent him from raping her. Simultaneously with Rufus's death, Dana experiences the "terrible, wrenching sickness" of her Middle Passage travels between past and present (*Kindred* 260). Despite her weakened state, she manages to move Rufus's body off of hers before she travels through time, but his hand remains on her arm. Recounting the process of her return to 1976, Dana reports: "Something harder and stronger than Rufus's hand clamped down on my arm, squeezing it, stiffening it, pressing into it—painlessly, at first—melting into it, meshing with it as though somehow my arm were being absorbed into something. Something cold and nonliving" (*Kindred* 260–61). The "cold and nonliving" force that grasps Dana's arm and divides her body, permanently, between past and present corresponds to the bar in the system of signification, the bar of the Middle Passage. This bar, which indicates the separation of signifier and signified and, in this instance, the distance between the physical black body and cultural constructions of blackness, transforms Dana's arm—her body—into an object consumed by Rufus in 1831 and her wall in 1976.

Dana, thus, experiences not only temporal liminality but also subjective liminality: her pre–Middle Passage subjectivity exists throughout time, just as her post–Middle Passage objectification surpasses the limits of linear temporality. Time travel makes impossible the separation of past, present, and future states of being. Considering the relationship between temporality and identity, Lacey asserts that Dana "literally becomes a multiple subject, defined in and through both the past and the present" (72). Additionally, the future—which cannot be separated from other temporalities in the novel—defines Dana. For instance, Butler's novel, and Dana's story, begins at the end, after Dana returns to 1976 for the last time, without her left arm. While Lisa Long argues that in killing Rufus, Dana "literally kills her past" (470), and Lacey asserts that with Dana losing an arm, "History has taken a piece of Dana's body" (72), the past remains alive for Dana, and the past, along with the present and future, permanently alters her identity. As such, Butler's novel draws a comparison between the blurred boundaries of time and being.

This liminal temporality and subjectivity accords with a posthuman multiple consciousness that makes possible an understanding of blackness in relation to the history of white supremacy and also beyond that history. Although Dana finds herself, like other black women, men, and children, oppressed regardless of the time period she inhabits, Butler's temporal and subjective disturbances indicate not the inevitability of antiblack violence but the potential for black freedom, including the freedom from the "transcendental signifier" of whiteness (Fuss 22). Steinberg argues that by depicting time as a circle or "zigzag," "Butler creates an historical possibility of the perception of self (and how it might be affected by matters of possession and ownership)" (472, 475). In addition to inspiring perceptions of the self as determined by dominating forces, liminal temporality encourages Butler's characters and readers to acknowledge subjectivities free from domination as well.

With his black nihilist theory, Warren presents the possibility of blackness as distinct from whiteness, although he positions both the achievement and product of this altered state of being as beyond comprehension. Considering, first, the dismantling of white supremacist systems, Warren rejects historical strategies for emancipation, arguing that "every emancipatory strategy that attempted to rescue blackness from anti-blackness inevitably reconstituted and reconfigured the anti-blackness it tried to eliminate" (239). Likewise, he dismisses future-focused solutions, since the promise of a more egalitarian future only promotes the continuation of struggle (Warren 233). In his philosophy of black nihilism, Warren advocates for the rejection of political action in the present as a tactic through which to separate black identity from the American Dream and Western metaphysics. He states, "Black nihilism demands a traversal, but not the traversal that reintegrates 'the subject' (and Being) back into society by shattering fundamental fantasies of metaphysics, but a traversal that disables and invalidates every imaginative and symbolic function" (240). "Because anti-blackness infuses itself into every fabric of social existence," Warren asserts, positioning the black subject outside of white supremacist systems "becomes something like *death* for the world," which makes sense, if, as he argues, divorcing the black subject from white supremacy "disables and invalidates every imaginative and symbolic function" we know (239, 240). Nevertheless, Warren pushes for a black nihilism that resists statements of purpose or progress, a nihilism that seeks to destroy white supremacy by denying the resuscitation of the past and the hope for the future that have, unwittingly, maintained the systems they seek to move beyond.

Yet temporality proves as slippery in Warren's "Black Nihilism and the Politics of Hope" as it does Butler's *Kindred*. Despite Warren's explicit rejection of "[p]rogress" and "futurity" (218), his philosophy fails to extricate itself from the language of Western metaphysics and, specifically, ideas of linear temporality: he must provide background and arrive, despite his protestations, at a "point" by the end of the article (243). However, Warren acknowledges the impossibility of his project: he gets as close to articulating a nonlinear theory of black nihilism—a theory that "does not extinguish hope but reconfigures it"—as semiotics and the conventions of academic writing allow (244). If, as Warren acknowledges, we cannot yet articulate or perhaps even imagine a reconfigured hope, then perhaps the key to freedom lies not in the rejection of temporality but the embrace of it. For instance, if we should not dismiss black suffering by simply hoping for a future more empowering than our present, why should we dismiss emancipation projects by anticipating a future as oppressive as our present? In the tradition of Du Bois and Fanon, who introduce ideas of liminal subjectivity that posthumanists have now applied to all individuals, regardless of race, and Eshun, who considers liminal temporality and subjectivity together, the theory of posthuman blackness provides a view of black subjectivity related to but also distinct from the linear trajectories of Western metaphysics.

Articulating a multiple consciousness rooted in posthumanism that allows for a view of blackness as connected to but discrete from white supremacy proves difficult. Because the posthuman lines of connection that link the subject to other people, periods, and powers undergo constant transformation, the subject exists in a continual state of development. Thus, while historical and contemporary white supremacies shape the black subject—and, as posthumanism necessitates and Warren corroborates, the black subject shapes white supremacies—the systems and the subject must be recognized as separate from one another. Posthuman multiple consciousness, such as that introduced by Eshun and explicated here, describes the ability to recognize the relationship between individual entities as well as the fluid nature of the relationship and the entities themselves. Theoretically this consciousness exists; however, can we imagine blackness, whiteness, or any identity divorced from white supremacy, when white supremacy shapes all that we know? If we can, we must turn away from what we know in order to achieve this posthuman multiple consciousness. By considering power relations in worlds outside of ours—such as the alien environment of Butler's "A Necessary Being" (2014)—we can envision and, perhaps, attain the impossible: the recognition of racial connection but rejection of racial subsumption.

"A Necessary Being" exists as both one of Butler's first and last neo–slave narratives, given that she wrote the novella early in her career but her estate published the text after her death in 2006. The story "depicts a crucial event in the backstory of her disavowed novel *Survivor*" (1978): the coming together of two alien tribes (Canavan). Set in an alternative world populated by the Kohn, "A Necessary Being" addresses the physical and emotional toll of captivity on members of the Hao, a rare ruling class revered by the Kohn for their perceived ability to "assure the people of good luck, fulfillment of their needs." While the Hao people's brilliant blue skin gives them power over all decisions in their Kohn communities, they have no authority over the rules of succession. K. Tempest Bradford explains that in the novella, "leadership is biologically determined and leaders are utterly necessary to the proper functioning of society, even when they are unwilling and forced into it." Accordingly, when in need of a new Hao leader, the Kohn steal a Hao from another region and cripple the Hao to limit the possibility of escape from the Kohn community: another instance of a Middle Passage. However, Butler's protagonist in "A Necessary Being," Tahneh, escapes this immobilization by being born of a crippled Hao and reared in the desert Rohkohn community. Tahneh's indoctrination makes her loyal to the desert people, but her inability to produce a suitably blue heir leads to the inciting incident of the novella: the capture and Middle Passage transport of Diut, the Hao of the mountain Tehkohn.

Similarities and differences exist between the alien world of Butler's novella and the "New World" of the Americas created by slavery and colonialism (Glissant 160; Wynter, "Beyond" 643). Loichot notes that in Butler's science fiction, she often "imagines a postterrestrial world to move beyond racial difference" (49). Yet rather than creating a "post-racial humanity," which Loichot identifies in Butler's earlier-published texts (50), Butler develops in "A Necessary Being" a hyper-racial world featuring extraterrestrial elements that disallow easy parallels between Kohn and human societies. While in the story skin color accords with varying levels of societal power, which parallels racism and colorism in the Americas, blue, yellow, and green skin and chameleonlike camouflage differentiate Hao and Kohn bodies from human bodies. Although Butler "addresses race and class head-on as well as in metaphorical terms" (Bradford), she also confounds contemporary hierarchies with her portrayal of the alien species: the unique "pure blue" flesh of the Hao grants them leader status, but their flesh also marks them as slaves to the Kohn. Because the Kohn revere the Hao as leaders but also subject them to violence and captivity, neither Kohn nor Hao beings occupy a power position like that of whites in white supremacist societies.

The dissimilarity of Kohn and American cultures allows Butler's readers to understand the Hao both in relation to and separate from the Kohn who place them in captivity, even if this posthuman multiple consciousness may be more difficult when considering social ties—and, specifically, race relations—in America. The novella's protagonist models multiple consciousness for Butler's readers. Tahneh understands how the Kohn see her, and she works to meet their expectations. For example, when a hunter expresses pride in representing his caste well, the narrator notes that Tahneh's body "whited and became slightly luminescent" as "a sign of the approval that she should have felt, but did not feel." Later, Tahneh rejects her "impulse to let her own body whiten with pleasure" when she achieves a political goal, knowing that to do so would make her fellow Hao, Diut, look weak to members of his Kohn community. Tahneh's knowledge of her desired actions and her decision to behave otherwise show that, one, she understands what the Kohn presume of the Hao (leadership and devotion) and, two, she exists both within and outside of these conventions.

Beyond demonstrating a double or triple consciousness that allows her to recognize her body's signification in Kohn culture and her awareness of her move from subject to object in this system, Tahneh achieves a post-human multiple consciousness with which she can understand herself as outside of not only Kohn conventions but also the Kohn system of signification. Warren argues that only by working outside of white cosmologies does black emancipation become possible, since efforts for freedom made within the white supremacist systems merely reinforce those systems. If, as Audre Lorde states, "the master's tools will never dismantle the master's house" (112), then Butler and other black women writers must "enlist the tools of power, books, pen" and "write history in which the former master/father is turned powerless" (Loichot 47). In "A Necessary Being," freedom—specifically, Hao liberation from threats of abduction and violence—can only be achieved through the destruction of the Kohn system of signification.

Initially, though, Tahneh and Diut appear to use the master's tools to dismantle the master's house. In order to prevent Diut's capture, Tahneh uses her influence to persuade her Rohkohn community and Diut, as well as his two Tehkohn compatriots, to join tribes rather than continue the tradition of fighting for Hao leaders. She states, "Diut, if we're superior people at all, we should be able to find a way to stop [your crippling or death] from happening." Despite the tradition of Hao being left out of succession discussions, Tahneh assures him, "My people will do what I tell them. Exactly what I tell them," and, as she predicts, the Rohkohn agree to move to the mountains with the Tehkohn. Tahneh and Diut work within the system by assuming the leadership positions bestowed upon them by the Kohn and using their power to alter the rules that have stood for generations.

However, in addition to wielding the master's tools, the Hao convey their awareness that changing tradition overlaps with the disintegration of Kohn metaphysics. During her efforts to bring together Rohkohn and Tehkohn, Tahneh notices her Kohn leaders being persuaded by her argument: "Tahneh had been waiting for this. It was an expression of the kind of belief, the kind of faith that made the people consider the Hao so essential. The

Hao were supposed to possess some special ability to bring good to their people. It was not just that they tried to give good government, promote unity. Their mere presence was supposed to assure the people of good luck, fulfillment of their needs. Why else would a captive Hao, a bitter cripple, be better than no Hao at all?" Tahneh's assertion that the Hao "*were supposed* to possess" (emphasis mine) a unique quality associated with unity and luck reveals her disbelief in the signified meaning of blue flesh. She situates her view of herself and other Hao leaders outside of the Kohn system of signification.

Diut similarly disregards Kohn ideas of Hao power by positioning Hao superiority as constructed rather than essential. Faced with Tahneh's idea to join their tribes, Diut "visualize[s] himself before his council of judges," seeking their approval rather than giving them orders. Later, when learning that Tahneh intends for him to serve as a "hostage among the Rohkohn that would ensure Rohkohn safe passage" to the mountain lands, Diut again sets aside his leadership position. While Tahneh hopes he will respond to the news of his hostage status by affirming her orders with his people, Diut flashes yellow—the color of "anger" but also submission—and acknowledges, within earshot of the Tehkohn, Tahneh's distrust of him and his people. Diut conveys the anger and fear felt by his captured Tehkohn friends rather than the superiority modeled by Tahneh. By demonstrating kinship with the Tehkohn, Diut weakens the transcendental signifier of Hao power and dismisses Kohn ontology.

Of course, as a "prequel to" or "deleted scene from" *Survivor* (Canavan), "A Necessary Being" exceeds the temporality in which Butler sets the story. Like *Kindred*, then, the ramifications of power hierarchies continue into the present and future: Tahneh and Diut fail to produce a Hao heir and find other Kohn and, later, human mates, and the merged Rohkohn and Tehkohn face Garkohn invasions (Canavan). As Gerry Canavan asserts in his review of the story, "those who have actually read *Survivor* [. . .] will recognize the characteristically Butlerian sour note" to the "very traditional sort of 'happy ending'" of "A Necessary Being." However, the shifting tenor of the novella, when considered in the context of the novel, does not diminish the multiple consciousness displayed within the text. While a starred review of the collection in *Kirkus Reviews* states that Tahneh "considers if [the Kohn] or the Hao are her true people," Butler rejects an easy binary; instead, Tahneh and Diut see themselves both as connected to and distinct from the Kohn.

The Hao neither rule over the Kohn, projecting their subjects as inferior, nor see themselves as beholden to Kohn superiors. Instead, Middle Passage experiences in the story, including the move of Hao leaders from one region to another and, more significantly, Tahneh and Diut's shift from enemies to allies, foster for the Hao a posthuman multiple consciousness that situates Hao identity within and outside of the ontology of Kohn power.

Tahneh and Diut's demonstration of posthuman multiple consciousness provides a path by which readers might discover a new way of thinking about being. Warren argues that the end of antiblack violence requires "a traversal that disables and invalidates every imaginative and symbolic function" (240). Posthuman multiple consciousness might be that traversal—a crossing that can heal some of the wounds of the original Middle Passage—and science fiction gives readers strategies for achieving a multiple consciousness that crosses boundary lines and imagines new systems. As James Gunn and Karen Hellekson assert, science fiction functions as "the literature of change" because of its concern with that which is new, whether "new problems to deal with or new perspectives on old problems" (x). Otherworldly or alien texts, including Butler's *Wild Seed, Kindred*, and "A Necessary Being"—as well as more traditional fictions that contain speculative elements, such as Toni Morrison's *Beloved* (1987) and Julie Dash's *Daughters of the Dust* (1991)—allow readers to consider alternative routes by which to address not only the "old problems" of the past but also those old problems that persist into the present. In these works, liminal temporalities and subjectivities come together to provide a posthuman perspective of our world. If, as Eshun argues, "The future is a much better guide to the present than the past" (*More* 00[–001]), then perhaps the alien is a much better guide to the human than we are ourselves.

CHAPTER 5

Submarine Transversality in
Texts by Sheree Renée Thomas and Julie Dash

At the opening of Sheree Renée Thomas's speculative short story "How Sukie Cross de Big Wata" (2003), the Earth's waters tell about an encounter with a child named Stella, later called Sukie Diamond, on the banks of the Mississippi River.[1] The narrator communicates with Stella through "muddy waters" that ask her if she knows the river (327). By issuing a "cold current swirling round her toes" and a "warm current to tickle the blackbottom of her feet," the waters also question Stella about her history and her relationship with her mother (327). The literally fluid language of the story indicates that although Stella stands at the banks of the Mississippi as an escaped slave, she must be understood as linked to other places, times, and states of being: her history and subjectivity are liminal.

Liminality, or the state of existing on a threshold, describes not only Stella but also many other characters in contemporary women's neo–slave narratives, including Sethe from Toni Morrison's *Beloved* (1987), Dessa from Sherley Anne Williams's *Dessa Rose* (1986), Dana from Octavia E. Butler's *Kindred* (1979), and Unborn Child from Julie Dash's *Daughters of the Dust* (1991). Despite being situated in an historical setting, these characters experience events and encounter beings from beyond the confines of logical space and time—especially when they are written into works of speculative historical fiction. Lauren J. Lacey asserts that authors of speculative fiction rely on characters, settings, or events unfamiliar in our "real" world in order to blur the boundaries between the possible and impossible. Lacey argues that contemporary speculative fiction texts "incorporate elements of the fantastic (such as time travel, the ability to fly, and even fairy tale figures) in ways that redefine the relationship between the past and present so that the past becomes a site of possibility rather than a closed story" (19). By confounding linear, rational notions of space and time, fantastic elements offer alternative trajectories for the dispersal of power, a proposition particularly promising for the oppressed.

In black women's speculative historical fiction, fantastic elements do not simply disrupt rationality; instead, these elements indicate that we must dismiss reason as a—or, more importantly, the—hallmark of human identity. Both Thomas's short story "How Sukie Cross de Big Wata" and Dash's film *Daughters of the Dust* reject theories of rational subjectivity founded in the recognition of difference by featuring children who develop through their connections to others. Thomas's Stella uses her own power to emerge from the womb after her pregnant mother's death, but her bond with her mother affords her the ability to walk, talk, and spit fire immediately upon her entrance into the world. Dash's protagonist, unnamed on screen but referred to as Unborn Child in the screenplay, similarly disrupts the notion that subjectivity develops from the separation of self and other by operating as a bridge figure throughout the film, aiding her family members in understanding the links between past, present, and future. Both texts establish black identity as founded in posthuman liminality and, in doing so, disturb hierarchies that would position black subjects as less-than-human.

Prioritizing liminal connections over rational dislocations requires a move away from white, Eurocentric theories of psychosexual development. A black posthumanist understanding of identity formation develops from Caribbean- and Afrocentric theories, including Martinican poet, novelist, and theorist Édouard Glissant's notion of the submarine and Jamaican theorist and dramatist Sylvia Wynter's expansion of Glissant's work into a "New Discourse of the Antilles" (Wynter, "Beyond" 639).[2] Investigating liminal, posthumanist space and time with the aid of Glissant and Wynter establishes not only the necessity of black posthumanist readings of neo–slave narratives but also the necessity of black posthumanist readings of existing theories—including posthuman theory itself. A black posthumanist approach to identity formation offers an alternative to deracialized and dehistoricized theories of psychosexual development and posthuman subjectivity. By positioning liminality as the hallmark of identity, oppressed peoples, including black subjects, become the "human" of "posthumanism." Black posthuman theory thus enacts liminality, emerging from a future-based correction of an historical oversight by which white, liberal humanist notions of being became foundational to understandings of humanity and subjectivity.

REJECTING REASON:
GLISSANT'S SUBMARINE

In his theories of postcolonial Caribbean identity, place, and space, Glissant anticipates the emergence of the black posthuman subject. Like contemporary Afrofuturist theorist Kalí Tal—who points out that "African American critical theory provides very sophisticated tools for the analysis of cyberculture, since African American critics have been discussing the problem of multiple identities, fragmented personae, and liminality for over a hundred years"—Glissant turns to the historical experiences of the oppressed in order to provide an account of the origins of liminal identity. The similarity of both theorists' views of identity shows that Glissant offers a preview of the black posthuman subject.

Glissant, like Tal, argues that black identity forms through the convergences of multiple spaces and times. Accordingly, he rejects colonial constructions of history, asserting instead that Caribbean temporalities exist "fixed in the void of an imposed nonhistory" that resulted when a group of people came into place—and came into being—due to the slave trade (64). The postcolonial "nonhistory" results in a Caribbean past located in the present and future:

> The past, to which we were subjected, which has not yet emerged as history for us, is, however, obsessively present. The duty of the writer is to explore this obsession, to show its relevance in a continuous fashion to the immediate present. This exploration is therefore related neither to a schematic chronology nor to a nostalgic lament. It leads to the identification of a painful notion of time and its full projection forward into the future, without the help of those plateaus in time from which the West has benefited, without the help of that collective density that is the primary value of an ancestral cultural heartland. That is what I call *a prophetic vision of the past*. (Glissant 63–64)

Glissant's "*prophetic vision of the past*" signals that the slave trade did not merely disrupt Caribbean history; instead, slavery created a liminal temporality for the Caribbean subject (64). While projecting oppressive histories into the future proves "painful," Glissant argues that writers must chart alternative postcolonial chronologies in order to understand not only Caribbean time but also Caribbean identity (64–65).

Glissant extends temporal, spatial, and subjective liminality from the Caribbean to the Americas based on the similar colonial experiences of Caribbean and "New World" black subjects (160). In her translation of Glissant, Wynter explains that because Caribbean and American black societies "'did not pre-exist the colonial act, but were literally the creation of that act,' one cannot 'speak of structures disturbed by colonialism, of traditions that have been uprooted'" ("Beyond" 643). While other colonized groups could attempt "a return, after independence, to the old ancestral bases of identity, on which to meet the challenge of coping with a contemporary reality," the formerly enslaved in the Caribbean and Americas enjoyed no such local history divorced from oppression (Wynter, "Beyond" 643). Accordingly, Caribbean and American black subjects alike must embrace Glissant's prophetic visions of the past if they wish to escape the colonial version of history imposed upon them.

Accepting a prophetic view of the past allows the colonized not only to escape colonial histories but also to integrate liminality into black identity and culture. Glissant contends that the temporally liminal histories of black Caribbean and American subjects "bring to light an unsuspected, because it is so obvious, dimension of human behavior: transversality" (66). *Transversality*, a term popular in geometry, describes the intersectional quality of lines or of networks of lines. Glissant's transversal subjectivity, like Deleuze and Guattari's rhizomatic structure of knowledge, releases the individual from "the linear, hierarchical vision of a single History that would run its unique course" (Glissant 66). Rather than being consumed by a colonial history, Caribbean and New World black subjects experience multiple, intersecting histories that interrupt the lasting power of a colonial past.

With his prophetic and transversal vision of the black experience, Glissant allows the historical black subject an intersectionality that prefigures contemporary posthuman liminality. Specifically, Glissant's theory of submarine identity serves as a precursor to posthuman subjectivity. Borrowing from Caribbean poet and historian Kamau Brathwaite, who asserts in his assessment of scholarship on Caribbean history, "The unity is submarine" (qtd. in Glissant 66), Glissant perceives in the black Caribbean subject "[s]ubmarine roots: that is floating free, not fixed in one position in some primordial spot, but extending in all directions in our world through its network of branches" (67). Ian Baucom clarifies the relationship between self and space in Glissant's notion of the submarine, asserting that Glissant imagines a "heterotopic self" situated in "an equally fluid environment" that "not only encompasses the subject but 'passes through' it" (par. 7). As Ruth Mayer and Yogita Goyal argue, Glissant's submarine envelops liminal notions of not only space, as the discussion of unfixed positions suggests, but also time. Mayer states that when placed in contrast to "the chartered and mapped high seas, this world below emerges as a realm beneath existing lines of power and signification, an ambivalent space, [. . .] a fantasy space which is always as much of the future as it is of the past" (561). Goyal similarly promotes the transversality of Glissant's notion of the submarine by stating that the "subliminal roots" Glissant theorizes "are constantly being created rather than located in a single primordial moment" (238).

Glissant brings ideas of multiple locations and times together by commenting on the significance of contemporary understandings of black experiences during slavery. He writes that Brathwaite's evocation of the "submarine" "can only evoke all those Africans weighed down with ball and chain and thrown overboard whenever a slave ship was pursued by enemy vessels and felt too weak to put up a fight. *They sowed in the depths the seeds of an invisible presence.* And so transversality, and not the universal transcendence of the sublime, has come to light. It took us a long time to learn this. We are the roots of a cross-cultural relationship" (66–67). According to Glissant's theory, the enslaved subjects who "*sowed in the depths the seeds of an invisible presence*" remain extant despite their historical deaths. As Glissant, Baucom, Mayer, and Goyal argue, the submarine depths are about the present and future—that which grows from the seeds sown—as well as the past.

Transversality rather than transcendence characterizes black Caribbean and American subjects during and after slavery. Given that transversality encompasses colonial and anticolonial as well as racist and antiracist understandings of the past, present, and future, Glissant's submarine theory applies to the contemporary posthuman subject as well. By crafting a theory of identity linked to historical and contemporary experiences of liminality, Glissant offers a posthumanist approach to posthuman theory. Accepting a fluid, transversal, and liminal posthuman identity demands that the historical subject be unmoored from a fixed past, which includes white humanist notions of humanity. Baucom asserts that Glissant's submarine theory works toward this task, given that the author insists "that we free ourselves from those acts of forgetting upon which the constitution of fixed identities so regularly depend, but asks that in joining ourselves to the no-longer forgotten we refuse to fetishize an alternate past and instead cultivate a vulnerability to the mutating ebb-tides of submarine memory" (par. 6). Glissant, according to Baucom, pushes his readers to look to the past but also to recognize the influence of multiple temporalities on the memory. By rejecting concretized histories, memories, and identities, Glissant refuses to prioritize liberal humanism over alternative ways of being and theorizing. As such, his submarine theory stands as a posthumanist mechanism—and, in particular, a black posthumanist mechanism—for understanding the posthuman subject.

Glissant must be counted among those theorists speaking on posthuman liminality in that he answers the call for a "(post) humanism that does not privilege European Man and its idiom" (Jackson 673). Wynter best explicates Glissant's rejection of the liberal humanist European Man by arguing that his works fight against reason. She describes the "major themes of Glissant's works as performative acts of countermeandering directed against the semantic character or behavior-regulating program, instituted by our present order of discourse and therefore by its related order of rationality or mode of 'conventional' or cultural 'reason'" ("Beyond" 639). Wynter maintains that within our current order of discourse (i.e., our system of naming and categorizing), which defines the rational subject by means of its antithesis to the irrational Other, the black African or Caribbean individual comes to stand as "the Negative Signifier" of white, European Man ("On Disenchanting" 222–23, 237). She asserts that Glissant's central themes, which include "history," "psychic disorder and cultural malaise," "consumerism," and hierarchical ordering, participate in the destruction of the dominant discourses committed to binary linguistic and ontological structures ("Beyond" 639–40). If the rational self—the white, liberal humanist subject—cannot be understood as the subject of Glissant's submarine being, then a new type of identity emerges: one as relational and fluid as the submarine itself. By joining Wynter in recognizing "differing modes of the human" (Wynter, "On Disenchanting" 241), Glissant predicts a new type of subject that overlaps or corresponds with the black posthuman subject and, in doing so, provides a prophetic black posthumanist vision of posthumanism.

SUBMARINE ROOTS IN
SHEREE RENÉE THOMAS'S
"HOW SUKIE CROSS DE BIG WATA"

As Wynter argues, Glissant's theories of Caribbean liminality—including the need for a *"prophetic vision of the past"*—apply to the black American subject. In Thomas's "How Sukie Cross de Big Wata," free-floating views of temporality and subjectivity allow Stella/Sukie to exceed the history of enslavement into which Thomas situates her. Additionally, the story's liminal views of the self confound white, liberal humanist notions of subjectivity, particularly traditional understandings of psychosexual development. Thomas's story depicts a submarine transversality that extends beyond the depths of the ocean to the waters of the Mississippi. In the story, all bodies of water—even those seemingly rooted in place or to person, such as the amniotic fluid of the womb—exemplify the rootlessness of the submarine.

As described above, the line of questioning generated by the Earth's waters in Thomas's story draws attention to the transversality of both external and internal bodies of water. By first asking Stella if she knows the river and second inquiring about her relationship with her mother, the narrator links the Mississippi and the womb, indicating that both have enveloped Stella but also that both move her beyond the specific location in which she can be found. Moreover, the Earth's waters position Stella and her enslaved ancestors within the transversal womb of time—and thus outside of linear, colonial history—given their existence as "the creation of [the colonial] act" (Wynter, "Beyond" 643). The narrator places Stella's ancestors' origin at "the door of no return" (the entrance of the slave ship) and their passage across the water to "the land they call mother" (their home in America). Given this modern, water-based birth story, Stella's mother and ancestors, as well as Stella herself, must be understood as subjects with submarine roots, individuals "not fixed in one position in some primordial spot, but extending in all directions in our world" through their connectedness to external and internal fluidities (Glissant 67).

In some ways, reading connection as inherent to Stella's subjectivity seems incongruous with the events that take place early in Thomas's story. The narrator indicates that Stella's power and personality reveal themselves only after her mother's death, a parting that mimics the traditional Lacanian paradigm of psychosexual development, particularly the imperative that the child must separate from the mother in order to enter into the symbolic order. While the narrator mentions Stella in the opening of the tale—speaking, for instance, of her many names and ability to "steal away"—she does not emerge as a full-fledged character until her separation from her mother, a moment marked not by her birth but her mother's death: "Folks say they could see her little arms and legs just a waving under the cold dead flesh of her mama. Say Stella birth herself in her own time, say she come on out kicking, and swinging too, and been swinging ever since" (Thomas 327–28). By contrasting Stella's animated limbs with her mother's "cold dead flesh" even when Stella resides within her mother's womb, Thomas's narrator emphasizes the protagonist's physical dissimilarity from her mother. Such descriptions reveal that Stella's difference from her mother—as opposed to her transversal links to the surrounding world—prompts her emergence as the protagonist of the narrator's story.

Likewise, Stella's entrance into language, the realm of symbols and signs, initially appears to be spurred by her separation from her mother and community. Thomas's narrator reports that in the moments after leaving her mother's womb, Stella expresses, first, her dissimilarity from her mother and, second, her desire to distance herself from those who surround her: "Stella leaned back, took in her world, saw her mama tree-stump dead—the spirit still fresh on her breath—and didn't drop no tears. No, Stella didn't cry. Stella leaned back, smacked the old granny that held her, and snatched back her navel string. Say she'd bury it her own damned self. Say she'd rather carry her destiny in her own hands than trust it to some strange bloodtree, cut down 'fore its roots can grow, like her mama and all her kin that come before" (Thomas 328). When read through Julia Kristeva's concept of the abject, Stella's violent reaction to the sight of her mother's body—her smack of the woman who holds her—and her expressed desire to gain distance from those who witnessed her birth can be understood as part of her struggle to identify herself as separate from the (m)other (13). Although Stella links herself to her mother by taking possession of the umbilical cord, the context of her actions—readers learn repeatedly that she "leaned back," distancing herself from those around her—appears antithetical to Glissant's ideas of intersectionality.

Despite her separation from her mother and community, Thomas's protagonist departs from the traditional stages of psychosexual development and demonstrates, through her reliance on maternal, nonrepresentational speech, a liminal or transversal identity. The narrator positions Stella's speech within the realm of the mother rather than the father by comparing her words to those her mother spoke during Stella's last moments in the womb. Stella's mother speaks in "spirit-tongue," a language "part African, part Indian" that few understand because "ain't nobody live long enough to know the meaning to" the words (Thomas 331, 327). Stella, like her mother, communicates using spirit language; after her birth, Stella "remembered what most forget, on the trip to this world from the next," which allows her to speak "in spirit-tongue, as her mama before her death" (Thomas 329, 331). Thomas's narrator asserts that Stella recalls from her time in the womb the language she heard her mother speak, and she uses this maternal language to keep her connection with her mother alive. Stella's words not only blur subjective boundaries between Stella and her ancestors, but they also blur spatial and temporal boundaries, since only the dead—those not of this world—or the old and newly born understand the language.

Fluency in spirit-tongue distinguishes Stella from "rhetorical man" and his "historico-phenomenological space of being/discourse" predicated on difference (Wynter, "On Disenchanting" 214). Stella instead inhabits a transversal submarine state, where an acknowledgment of connection—between African and Indian, dead and living, past and present—precipitates communication. According to Glissant, nonrepresentational language—such as Stella's spirit-tongue—links transversal identities, spaces, and times: "The word as uncertainty, the word as whisper, noise, a sonorous barrier to the silence imposed by darkness. The rhythm, continuously repeated because of a peculiar sense of time. Time, which needs to be undated. Opaqueness is a positive value to be opposed to any pseudo-humanist attempt to reduce us to the scale of some universal model. We welcome opaqueness, through which the other escapes me, obliging me to be vigilant whenever I approach. We would have to deconstruct French to make it serve us in all these ways. We will have to structure Creole in order to open it to these new possibilities" (187). While Glissant's Martinican speech echoes Kristeva's choric communication in that both emphasize "rhythm, tone, colour, with all that which does not simply serve for representation" (Gallop 124), Glissant works outside of white culture's psychoanalytic theories of language. Rosi Braidotti argues that Glissant's demand for a "hybridized poly-lingualism" fights against Eurocentric systems by offering "an affirmative answer to the coercive mono-culturalism imposed by the colonial and imperial powers" (133).

In Thomas's story, for instance, spirit language fights against "coercive mono-culturalism" in that it rejects differentiation in favor of association: rather than establishing linguistic parameters through the contradistinction of self and other, Stella's language connects her to her mother and ancestors in the past as well as her community in the present.

In addition to offering a critique of white, Eurocentric views of language, the move from separation to association also suggests that psychoanalytic theories fail to capture the development of the black subject. Embracing alternative conceptions of the human—including the posthuman—requires new theories of the self. The problem with current trends lies in their assumption of a universal human identity based on the white, liberal humanist subject.[3] Glissant deconstructs acultural notions of the human subject by offering multiple, local, and liminal views of human identity. In particular, Wynter argues, Glissant situates the black subject outside of the symbolic realm of reason: "Glissant's Antillean human subject, coming to realize its cognitive autonomy not merely with respect to its knowledge of physical and organic nature but with respect to its knowledge of itself as a mode of life which exists *outside* the symbolic circuit of organic life, must therefore now accept the full responsibility of its position as a 'free outcast' who confronts 'the rest of nature as a trial, task, issue and enigma, as an alien abode,' and therefore as the causal source of our own Good, our own Evil" ("Beyond" 645–46). While Wynter asserts that Glissant's transversal subjects must establish their own system of ethics—they must, as Donna Haraway implores of the cyborg, take "pleasure in the confusion of boundaries" and "responsibility in their construction" (150)—an Antillean ethics relieves transversal subjects from colonial modes of being.

By working against reason to offer alternative figurations of human identity, Glissant's submarine transversality anticipates posthuman liminality. In lieu of viewing separation as necessary to the advent of subjectivity, the submarine subject, like the posthuman being, develops out of connections to or relations with others. Alexander G. Weheliye similarly asserts that according to Glissant's theory, "Relation is not a waste product of established components; rather, it epitomizes the constitutive potentiality of a totality that is structured in dominance and composed of the particular processes of bringing-into-relation, which offer spheres of interconnected existences that are in constant motion" (*Habeas* 12–13). According to Glissant's theory, the connections that grow out of colonial nonhistories produce transversal notions of being in time (64). Moreover, Glissant's transversal temporality indicates that the idea of a "beginning" to subjectivity, as suggested in traditional psychoanalytic theories, is false: the "multiple converging paths" hidden in the depths of the submarine invalidate the idea of a single, linear temporality or rational subjectivity (66). By moving beyond bordered notions of space and time, Glissant positions liminality as inherent to the subject's identity.

In "How Sukie Cross de Big Wata," both language and subjectivity develop through connections to the mother and other members of the community, which places the black subject within the realm of the submarine rather than the symbolic. When Stella visits the belly hole she climbed out of at the moment of her birth, she hears or feels "somebody call her name": "The call echoed from the pit of her own belly, sound like sweet spirits sangin'. Then Sukie felt a kiss—soft full lips on her temple, the place where the spirit rest—and she knew it was her mama come to visit" (Thomas 332). Language, specifically her mother's call, originates from Stella's "belly," her womb. Thomas's repeated mentions of the waist/belly/womb emphasize Stella's connection to her mother throughout time: she carries near her womb—the site from which potential future generations might emerge—the umbilical cord that physically linked her to her mother in the past, and she feels the pull of her mother's ongoing presence in her womb as well.

Additionally, multiple references to fluid in the story, from the amniotic fluid of the womb to drinking water and rain, indicate a persistent connection between Stella and her mother. On her path to freedom, Stella comes across the overseer who beat her mother. The overseer looks "her up and down like he thirsty and want a taste," and Stella rejects his advances by reminding him of her mother's resistant body. She asks the overseer, "[I]f you couldn't handle my mama [. . .] what make you think you can handle me?" (Thomas 328–29). Stella's question prompts the overseer to ask, "Who yo' mama, girl?", an inquiry that Stella takes as an invitation to bring to life the violence the overseer committed against her mother. Stella sets her conjure powers upon him, "pressing her full lips on his rusty jaw. Burnt off half his face" (Thomas 329). Stella's body and her mother's spirit join together to defeat their wrongdoer by making him understand their pain. Their kiss—part of the "taste" the overseer thirsts for—brings the overseer into their realm of connection, and he expresses his relationship to the women by shouting the same spirit-word Stella's mother yelled before her death:

"Steela!" (Thomas 329). The overseer's inability to imagine a world beyond the rational results in him drowning in his victims' submarine depths.

After the overseer cries out using spirit language, rain begins to fall. The baptismal rain—another marker of the submarine—signals Stella's rebirth or shift into a new life: a life outside of slavery, a life as a fully realized subject. From this moment forward in the story, the narrator transitions from calling the protagonist Stella to referring to her as Sukie, a name that has been associated with the lily, a flower symbolizing rebirth and resurrection. Although readers see a shift in Stella/Sukie's identity, Thomas shows through the repeated image of baptismal rain that any move away from the mother and maternal body can only be understood as temporary and that the mother–child bond persists in the child's future.

Sukie and her mother commune in the submarine waters of the rain after Sukie returns to the scene of her birth. Sukie carries her mother's body with her on the journey out of Mississippi, but rain begins to dissolve the corpse: "Sukie [. . .] moved with heavy feet, allowing the black dirt so full of cottonseed, blood, and bone to fall heavily to the earth through her stiff fingers. She moved with purpose, flinging more of the black mud with each step, until all that remained of her mama's charred body were a few dark smudges on her fingertips and lips" (Thomas 333). While Sukie's continual movement, paired with her mother's disappearing body, suggest that she must distance and distinguish herself from her mother, Thomas once again rejects the mandate that subjectivity include separation from the mother by drawing a comparison between the bodies of the two women. The remains of her mother's body on Sukie's "fingertips and lips" suggest an act of communion: Sukie's kiss or even consumption of her mother's body and spirit.

The bodily communion of self and mother enables, as Sukie's name indicates, a physical and spiritual rebirth to occur. Sukie's body does not dissolve in the rain, but Sukie follows her mother in transforming her body in order to achieve freedom. "Some folk say when Sukie got to the river," the narrator states, "she turned herself into a stone. You know the kind, smooth and polished and slick" (Thomas 333). Coming to the river's edge, a patty-roller picks up the stone and skips it across the Mississippi in frustration because he cannot find Sukie. Once on the other side, Sukie emphasizes her physical power as well as her connection to her mother by materializing in her own human body and, again, singing the spirit-song her mother sang before her death (Thomas 333–34). Sukie's submarine connection to her mother—which defies space and time—allows her to make her way to freedom.

By calling upon her mother and internalizing her mother's language and body, Sukie develops as a subject. Her connection empowers her. Keeping her mother with her both physically and metaphorically allows Sukie to move from Mississippi, where she exists as an enslaved object, toward free land, where she can fully exercise her subjectivity. Thomas's neo–slave narrative demonstrates via the depiction of transversal spatiality and temporality that the black subject develops through connections rather than separations.

TRANSVERSAL SUBJECTIVITY IN
JULIE DASH'S *DAUGHTERS OF THE DUST*

The submarine depths of the ocean and the womb likewise come together in Dash's critically acclaimed *Daughters of the Dust*, the first independent feature film with a theatrical release by an African American woman. Set in 1902 in Ibo Landing, a Gullah community located on an island inlet off the coasts of South Carolina and Georgia, and narrated by Eula and Eli Peazant's unborn daughter, Dash's *Daughters of the Dust* reveals that submarine transversality instead of rational dislocation facilitates the development of identity. The unfixed, "floating free" branches of Glissant's submarine root system reveal themselves in Dash's film through the Peazant family's links across space and time (Glissant 67). Unborn Child and her great-great-grandmother Nana Peazant repair family relationships as several members get ready to move north, and they unite in this connection-focused project with Unborn Child's mother, Eula Peazant, who strives to keep her immediate family together following her sexual assault. Dash reveals the timelessness of mother–child bonds as the key to each character's quest. Unborn Child, Nana, and Eula rely on their maternal bonds as they acknowledge the family's oppressive history and their potentially empowering future.

The transversality of the submarine presents immediately in the film's cinematography, which creates an alternative temporality—one founded in fluidity—that frees Dash's characters from a "linear, hierarchical vision of a single History" that forecasts their extinction (Glissant 66). By embracing a nonlinear style, playing with frame rates (Bambara xv), and communicating through musical expression and vocal "ululation" (Dash, "Making" 16;

Dash, *Daughters* 65), Dash moves beyond "documentary and ethnographic approaches that tend to objectify the Black subject as object" (Foster 49).[4] Gwendolyn Audrey Foster argues that the film's celebration of African diasporic community and identity hinges on the idea of continuation: Dash honors "the persistence of African cultures despite all colonial efforts of suppression and oppression" (70). As Foster notes, Dash and Arthur Jafa, the film's cinematographer, consciously promote the continuation of diasporic culture by relying on "Afrocentric aesthetics" in their narrative strategy (Dash and Baker 158). In telling the story as an African griot or "old relative would retell it, not linear but always coming back around" (Rule c17), Dash and Jafa create "an alternative universe of visual reference and cinematic procedures, one in which Black beauty has self-determining agency" (Tate and Jafa 90). The Gullah individual of *Daughters of the Dust*, like Glissant's Antillean subject, emerges from colonial origins and takes power in "the specificity of its own Creole language, its own landscape and lived existential history" (Wynter, "Beyond" 643).

Paradoxically, the specificity of Caribbean and New World black subjects, including the Gullah men and women of Dash's film, lies in transversality: identities develop through connections across space and time rather than through separations. Baucom argues that Glissant's submarine theory posits "a self which manifests itself not as an essence but as a meandering" (par. 7). Because this "meandering" submarine subjectivity rejects rootedness in a single type of being or historical precedent for identity, submarine subjectivity prioritizes connectedness over separateness and, accordingly, liminality over rationality. Wynter asserts that a connection-driven view of the self, as theorized by Glissant, Aimé Césaire, Frantz Fanon, and others, requires the destruction of the rational subject: "The new discourse of the Antilles therefore goes 'beyond the Word of Man' in that it is impelled to replace the latter's postulate of 'man as Man,' of an ontogenic subject, with that of an everywhere culturally relative—because rhetoric-discursively cum neurophysiologically instituted—mode of the human subject and therefore of the relativity also of its necessarily negatively invested mode of the Abject, of Ontological Lack, of the 'Negro' as a 'different kind of creature,' as the only group (as Césaire pointed out) excluded from human status within the symbolic logic of the Word of Man and of its absolute model of the human" ("Beyond" 645). Wynter finds that acultural understandings of human identity position as the abject other not only the mother, as argued in the typical

Lacanian paradigm, but all people of color. Accordingly, new understandings of community and culture as networked require new understandings of the development of the self.

The power Unborn Child derives from her connections to multiple people, places, and times becomes apparent in the graveyard scene. Unborn Child's efforts to bring her parents together in the cemetery culminates in a climactic moment of spiritual implantation: Unborn Child runs into her mother's open arms, joining her spirit and her mother's body. While the moment of Unborn Child's birth takes place off camera after the story concludes, she reveals her agency through her participation in this spiritual conception. Now within Eula's body, the power of Unborn Child's spirit inspires Eula to tell the story of the Peazant family, a story that encompasses their history as slaves, their freedom on the island, and their future off of it (Daughters 67). The story not only links mother and child, but it also allows the family's Ibo ancestors to commune with Eula and Eli. Eli overhears the story his wife tells and, with the aid of the ancestors Unborn Child has evoked, reenacts the tale of the Ibo people who walked on water (Daughters 68). By bringing her family in touch with their history, a past filled with pain yet containing hopeful promise for the future, Unborn Child propels her parents forward in their relationship, uniting them once again.

Events from the past and predictions for the future overlap in the figure of Unborn Child. From the moment her voice can be heard in the film, Dash's audience recognizes the ties that bind her to historical and contemporary maternal figures in her family. Unborn Child recalls in an off-screen voiceover that her story begins before her birth, in the days when Nana prays to the ancestors for help in keeping the family together (Daughters 7, 25). Unborn child states that "the old souls" heed Nana's prayers by "guid[ing] [Unborn Child] into the New World" (Daughters 6). While Unborn Child's link to her great-great-grandmother calls her to Ibo Landing before her birth, once there, she makes her presence known. Invisible to her family members, she appears to viewers in the form of "a five-year-old" girl "wearing an INDIGO-colored BOW in her hair" (Daughters 25). By having child actress Kai-Lynn Warren play Unborn Child, Dash positions the character as one who is connected to others on two levels. First, the audience associates her (a young child) as dependent upon adults, particularly maternal figures, for care. However, this manifestation of youth belies the mature work Unborn Child does in bringing her family together, which adds a second layer to her connectedness. She invisibly integrates herself into the Peazant family, first making Nana aware of her arrival (Daughters 25), then seeking similar recognition from her Aunt Haagar (Daughters 28), and finally leading her parents to the family graveyard where they reconnect with each other by remembering their shared past and conveying their mutual dreams for the future (Daughters 64–68).

Unborn Child's transversality—her image of youth but wisdom of age, her connection to the past as well as the future—allows her to shape her parents' lives, and it also joins her with another mother in Dash's film: Nana, the oldest living mother of the Peazant family and Unborn Child's "symbolic double" (Rody 63). Both Nana and Unborn Child operate as bridge figures in the film. Nana notes that for the Peazants, she is "the bridge that they crossed over on": "I was the tie between then and now. Between the past and the story that was to come" (Daughters 33). This complex, liminal position, addressed during the second half of the twentieth century by Cherríe Moraga, Gloria Anzaldúa, Audre Lorde, and other feminists of color, has roots in African Ibo culture. In notes written on the screenplay for Daughters of the Dust, Dash equates Unborn Child to the Ibo deity Elegba, whom she calls "the one we appeal to overcome indecision" (Daughters 25). In addition to his role as messenger, Elegba is the deity of crossroads and thresholds, the bridge between humans and gods (Willis 274; Pelton 127–33). In Dash's film, both Unborn Child and Nana fill this liminal position, helping their family members (living and dead) understand one another and join together to move back into the past or forward into the future, as need be.

However, as Moraga asserts in her preface to This Bridge Called My Back, being a liminal or bridge figure is not easy. "'A bridge gets walked over,'" she quotes Barbara Smith as saying, before adding her own refrain: "Yes, over and over and over again" (xv). The difficult and unending bridge work undertaken in Daughters of the Dust evokes the "painful" foresight of Glissant's "prophetic vision of the past" (Glissant 64). Unborn Child and Nana, as figures who embody Glissant's transversal temporality, help their family members understand that their colonial history carries forward into the future; this history, as Glissant notes, "comes to life with a stunning unexpectedness" (63). Unborn Child states in a voiceover that her story takes place during "an age of beginnings, a time of promises" (Daughters 32), but viewers also understand Daughters of the Dust as set in a time of conflict and change that requires constant negotiation. For Nana, the events taking place in the present remind her of her early life as a slave and the turmoil she felt then. She mourns her mother's physical absence in the present, as she also did in the past, and she fears that her family's future move north will lead to their emotional and spiritual abandonment of Peazant family values, particularly the value of togetherness. While Unborn Child and Nana understand the transversal quality of time, they still experience the trauma of temporal overlaps, given that black, postcolonial histories materialize "at the edge" of what Caribbean and New World black subjects "can tolerate" (Glissant 63).

For the New World black subjects of Dash's *Daughters of the Dust*, connections—particularly connections to the mother—make possible the difficult work of navigating times of transition. In her assessment of the "motherline," the tradition of nurturance that bonds mothers and children, Anglo-American theorist Naomi Ruth Lowinsky argues that the intergenerational bonds that make up the motherline defy rational, linear constructions of time: "The Motherline is not a straight line, for it is not about abstract genealogical diagrams; it is about bodies being born out of bodies. Envision the word *line* as a cord, a thread, as the yarn emerging from the fingers of a woman at the spinning wheel. Imagine cords of connection tied over generations. Like weaving or knitting, each thread is tied to others to create a complex, richly textured cloth connecting the past to the future" (12). Rather than simply shifting vertical lines of kinship and inheritance from a paternal to a maternal paradigm, the motherline focuses on the multidirectional threads of connection that link the child to many "mothers," including female and male blood relatives, family friends, and other caretakers. In Dash's film, the threads of the motherline connect characters to past, present, and future sources of maternal strength. For instance, as Eli struggles with his feelings about his wife's rape, he turns to Nana, his great-grandmother, for support. The two talk about his transition from a child who believed in the old ways and dreamt of a better life to an adult who is skeptical about tradition and fears what is to come. Nana tells him, "The ancestors and the womb . . . they're one, they're the same" (*Daughters* 20), a message about the connectedness of past and future that Unborn Child joins Nana in communicating to Eli.

Connections, particularly mother–child connections, as emphasized by the repeated references to the transversal space of the womb in the film, also aid Eula, who similarly turns to her mother for help with the problems facing her family. Eula tells her cousin, "I needed to see my Ma. I needed to talk to her. So I wrote her a letter, put it beneath the bed with a glass of water, and I waited. I waited, and my Ma came to me. She came to me right away" (*Daughters* 45). While Eula never reveals the content of her conversation with her deceased mother, viewers note that Eula has an appreciation for traditional ways of knowing, which contrasts sharply with her cousin's view that the "only way for things to happen or for people to change is to keep moving" (*Daughters* 47). For Eli and Eula, the mother teaches that forward movement requires an acknowledgment of what came before. Past, present, and future intertwine in *Daughters of the Dust*, and Dash communicates this liminality through the mother's unbroken connection to her children.

I find that Dash's vision of a networked submarine subjectivity comes through most clearly in the character of Nana Peazant. Shortly before her descendants' journey north, Nana leads the family in a religious ceremony designed to keep the family united despite the distance that might separate them. She creates a charm bag or "Hand" that contains a lock of her mother's hair as well as a lock of her own. Together, these bodily tokens symbolize the connectedness of the Peazant people. "There must be a bond," Nana states, "a connection, between those that go up North, and those who across the sea. A connection!" (*Daughters* 77). Nana asks her family members to kiss the Hand and commit to preserving this connection, an action that several of her family members reject because of their distaste for "primitive" traditions and adoption of Christian beliefs (*Daughters* 64). Although these family members position Nana's ceremony—and their Ibo ancestors—as remnants of a past that should be overcome, Nana's invocation of the ancestors serves to move the family forward. In the narrative exposition of the screenplay, Dash writes, "And like those old Ibos, Nana Peazant calls upon the womb of time to help shatter the temporal restrictions of her own existence—to become a being who is beyond death, beyond aging, beyond time" (86). "The womb of time"—the fluid or, to use Glissant's term, "submarine" space that creates an unceasing connection between mother and child, ancestor and descendant—allows Nana to live on in body in Ibo Landing but in spirit with her children in the North (*Daughters* 89). Like Stella, who in "How Sukie Cross de Big Wata" calls her mother forth from her womb, Nana's descendants will carry her spirit within them, providing Nana with new life and themselves with the "strength" that, according to Nana, accompanies her spirit's presence (*Daughters* 86).

Through her creation of characters that emphasize the ongoing bond between mother and child, Dash shows subjectivity as developing through connections to others—particularly mothers—across space and time. Caroline Rody argues that unlike other popular black women's narratives, *Daughters of the Dust* "demonstrates little anxiety about losing or recovering mothers. Contact with ancestors here, in contrast with *Beloved*, seems utterly assured, and daughterly desire for reunion completely fulfilled" (63). More than simply making reunion possible, Dash's film, like Thomas's short story, reveals that separation need not occur.

While the bonds between self and other do break in Thomas's and Dash's texts when slavery and colonialism physically divide families, reading the works through Glissant's submarine theory reveals that transversal connections remain across space and time. As Nana Peazant tells her descendants in *Daughters of the Dust*, "Take me wherever you go. I'm your strength" (86). Finding power in the presence of others, the children in these texts work before their births and well into adulthood to build better lives for themselves and their families.

Transversal submarine networks made physical by rivers, oceans, and wombs link the child protagonists to multiple temporalities. Thomas's and Dash's texts demonstrate that the child protagonists learn strategies for facing and embracing changes via their connections to others and, in particular, their mothers. However, locating power within the bonds that exist between mothers and children in diasporic cultures can be a dangerous project. As many theorists and critics point out, patriarchal and racist forces have historically worked to control women's bodies and subjectivities by mandating maternity and associating female identity with motherhood, particularly a self-effacing maternal ideal.[5] While contemporary analyses of the mother–child bond must acknowledge these historical constructions, they need not perpetuate them.

Black women's contemporary works of historical fiction offer a view of the future we need. These texts demonstrate an appreciation for maternal bonds as well as other forms of connection, including systems of communal care and solidarity. Black women's historical narratives—whether found in visual art, fiction, music, film, or other genres—demonstrate that links made across space and time empower black subjects, whether by offering them historical strategies for healing or new opportunities for resistance. In these works, black women in particular exceed the boundaries that would seek to contain them. As Dash states, "In my world, black women can do anything. They ride horses and fly from trapezes; they are in the future as well as in the past" (Rule C17). The theory of posthuman blackness helps us understand this temporal and subjective liminality as a source of both individual agency and collective authority.

NOTES

INTRODUCTION

1. Haraway joins Morrison, Tal, hooks, and Eshun in positioning black subjects—and, in particular, black women—as representative figures in her theorizing, but critics challenge her choice to group together dissimilar women of color as cyborgs solely on the basis of their shared outsider status. See Schueller, Sandoval, Puar, and Wilkerson for critiques of Haraway's reliance on women of color in her cyborg theorizing.

2. In the aftermath of Hurricane Katrina in 2005, the Superdome housed storm refugees. Reports of suffering in the Superdome—unsanitary living conditions, sexual violence, and food and water shortages—coupled with accusations of racism against the mainstream media and the Federal Emergency Management Agency (FEMA) indicate the confluence of race, gender, and class oppressions. The mothers in the video hold photos of their deceased sons, Trayvon Martin, Michael Brown, and Eric Garner, black men whose deaths became associated with the Black Lives Matter Movement.

3. Connecticut College presented An Afrofuturism Symposium in November of 2016; the New School hosted Afrofuturism: #Blackisviral in May 2016 and Afrofuturism: Designing New Narratives to Empower the African Diaspora in May 2015; New York University held the symposium Posthuman Futures in April 2016; Clark Atlanta University put on the symposium Ancient and New STE(A)M: Roots and Futures of Black Speculative Arts and Science Fictions in February of 2016; the University of Geneva in Switzerland organized Approaching Posthumanism and the Posthuman in June 2015; the Humanities Division at Essex County College put on Speculative Humanities: Steampunk to Afrofuturism in March 2015; Pomona and Scripps Colleges hosted Midnight Vistas, an Afrofuturism conference, in February 2015; and Loyola Marymount University organized the colloquium Astro-Blackness: Remaking and (Re) Mixing Black Identity Before, Now and Beyond in February 2014.

CHAPTER 1
Temporal Liminality in
Toni Morrison's Beloved and A Mercy

1. The reference to "Sixty Million and more" comes from Morrison's dedication at the beginning of *Beloved*.

2. See Beaulieu, O'Reilly, and Demetrakopoulos for more on the symbolic value of mother's milk in *Beloved*.

3. See Marianne Hirsch's *The Mother/Daughter Plot: Narrative Psychoanalysis, Feminism* (1989) for more on the disruption of relational triangles in *Beloved*.

4. Scholars differ on their assessments of Lina's position on Vaark's farm, with some referring to her as a "slave" (Moore 4; Wyatt, "Failed" 129) and others a "servant" or "worker" (Morgenstern 14). For more on the legal status of Native Americans during the colonial period, see Moore.

CHAPTER 2
Posthuman Solidarity in
Sherley Anne Williams's *Dessa Rose*

1. A Bay Area Rapid Transit (BART) police officer shot Grant while he was handcuffed and lying face down on the platform at the Fruitvale Station in Oakland, California, on January 1, 2009. A homeowner in Dearborn Heights, Michigan, a suburb of Detroit, shot McBride after she knocked on his door following a car crash on November 2, 2013.

2. The catchphrase "Hands up, don't shoot," along with the corresponding hands up gesture, developed following claims that Michael Brown had his hands raised and mouthed, "Don't shoot," to Darren Wilson moments before the officer shot him.

3. For more on the significance of Mammy as a character, as well as her influence on Rufel's development, see Rushdy, "Reading" and Rushdy, *Neo-Slave*.

4. For more information about Dinah, Dessa's real-life counterpart, see Davis.

CHAPTER 3
Afrofuturist Aesthetics in
the Works of Erykah Badu, Janelle Monáe, and Gayl Jones

1. For more information on Spratt's cover art, see Zoladz.

2. In *More Brilliant Than the Sun: Adventures in Sonic Fiction*, Eshun's style of pagination appears to mirror the track numbers and run time of audio recordings, with the negative numbers suggesting an interlude or preface. I cite his page numbers as they appear in his text.

3. See my article "Mama's Baby, Papa's Slavery? The Problems and Promise of Mothering in Octavia E. Butler's 'Bloodchild'" for more on Spillers's work and the link between historical and contemporary constructions of black identity.

CHAPTER 4
Posthuman Multiple Consciousness in
Octavia E. Butler's Science Fiction

1. Morrison discusses Middle Passage alienations in an interview with Paul Gilroy, published in Gilroy's *Small Acts: Thoughts on the Politics of Black Cultures*. Eshun notes that Tate's discussion of slavery and signification can be found in an unpublished in-

terview with Tate by Mark Sinker. My references to Tate come from Eshun's account of the interview in "Further Considerations on Afrofuturism."

CHAPTER 5
Submarine Transversality in
Texts by Sheree Renée Thomas and Julie Dash

1. Thomas published part of this story under the title "How Sukie Come Free" in volume 1, issue 1 of *Black Magnolias* (2001–02): 86–87.

2. Citations for Glissant refer to works from his collection *Caribbean Discourse: Selected Essays*.

3. For more on psychoanalytic readings of the black subject's psychosexual development, please see Spillers, Lillvis.

4. Citations for *Daughters* refer to the original page numbers of Dash's screenplay.

5. Hortense J. Spillers, Patricia Hill Collins, Gloria I. Joseph, and other theorists of the black family critique the white, Western model of the family in which the mother holds primary responsibility for childcare, arguing for, among other solutions, more equal parenting and altered social, political, and economic conditions for mothers. The collection *Double Stitch: Black Women Write about Mothers and Daughters* (1991), edited by Patricia Bell-Scott et al., provides a sound overview of mothering in the black family, including commentary on the power of black motherhood and constructions of community parenting.

WORKS CITED

Adams, Susan. "30 under 30: The Bright Young Stars of Art and Style." *Forbes* 17 Dec. 2012. Web. 10 Aug. 2015.

"All #BlackLivesMatter. This Is Not a Moment, but a *Movement*." About Us. Black Lives Matter. Web. 15 Aug. 2015.

Allen, Donia Elizabeth. "The Role of the Blues in Gayl Jones's *Corregidora*." *Callaloo* 25.1 (2002): 257–73. Web. 14 June 2011.

Altman, Alex. "The Short List: Black Lives Matter." *Time* 2015. Web. 1 June 2016.

Anatol, Giselle Liza. *The Things That Fly in the Night: Female Vampires in the Literature of the Circum-Caribbean and African Diaspora*. New Brunswick: Rutgers UP, 2015. Print. Critical Caribbean Stud.

Anders, Charlie Jane. "Black Kirby and Janelle Monáe: The New Cutting Edge of Afrofuturism." *io9*. Gawker Media, 1 Oct. 2013. Web. 24 July 2014.

Anzaldúa, Gloria. *Borderlands/La Frontera: The New Mestiza*. San Francisco: Aunt Lute, 1987. Print.

Appiah, Kwame Anthony. "Is the Post- in Postmodernism the Post- in Postcolonial?" *Critical Inquiry* 17.2 (1991): 336–57. Web. 11 Feb. 2012.

Badu, Erykah. "Gone Baby, Don't Be Long." *New Amerykah Part Two (Return of the Ankh)*. Universal Motown, 2010. Music Video. Dir. Flying Lotus. *YouTube*. 21 July 2014. Web.

———. "Next Lifetime." *Baduizm*. Kedar Records, 1997. Music Video. Dir. Erykah Badu and Troy Montgomery. *YouTube*. 21 July 2014. Web.

———. "On & On." *Baduizm*. Kedar Records, 1997. MP3.

———. "Window Seat." *New Amerykah Part Two (Return of the Ankh)*. Universal Motown, 2010. MP3.

Baker, Houston A. *Blues, Ideology and Afro-American Literature: A Vernacular Theory*. Chicago: U of Chicago P, 1984. Print.

Bambara, Toni Cade. Preface. Dash, *Daughters of the Dust: The Making* xi–xvi.

Barr, Marleen S., ed. *Afro-Future Females: Black Writers Chart Science Fiction's Newest New-Wave Trajectory*. Columbus: Ohio State UP, 2008. Print.

Basu, Biman. "Hybrid Embodiment and an Ethics of Masochism: Nella Larsen's *Passing* and Sherley Anne Williams's *Dessa Rose*." *The Commerce of Peoples: Sadomasochism and African American Literature*. Lanham: Lexington, 2012. Print.

Baucom, Ian. "Charting the 'Black Atlantic.'" *PMC* 8.1 (1997): n.p. Web. 30 Jan. 2015.

Beaulieu, Elizabeth Ann. *Black Women Writers and the American Neo-Slave Narrative: Femininity Unfettered*. Westport: Greenwood, 1999. Print. Contributions in Afro-American and African Studies 192.

Bell-Scott, Patricia, et al., eds. *Double Stitch: Black Women Write about Mothers and Daughters*. Boston: Beacon, 1991. Print.

Benjamin, Jessica. *The Bonds of Love: Psychoanalysis, Feminism, and the Problem of Domination*. New York: Pantheon, 1988. Print.

Beyoncé. *Lemonade*. Parkwood Columbia, 2016. Tidal.

Blumberg, Antonia. "NYC Clergy Join Black and Latino City Council Caucus 'Die In' to Protest Eric Garner Killing." *The Huffington Post*. The Huffington Post, 8 Dec. 2014. Web. 31 Dec. 2014.

Bouson, Brooks J. *Quiet as It's Kept: Shame, Trauma, and Race in the Novels of Toni Morrison*. Albany: State U of New York P, 2000. Print.

Bradford, K. Tempest. "An 'Unexpected' Treat for Octavia E. Butler Fans." Rev. of *Unexpected Stories*, by Octavia E. Butler. NPR Books 10 July 2014. Web. 6 July 2015.

Braidotti, Rosi. *The Posthuman*. Cambridge: Polity, 2013. Print.

Butler, Judith. *Gender Trouble: Feminism and the Subversion of Identity*. New York: Routledge Classics, 2006. Print.

Butler, Octavia E. "Bloodchild." *Bloodchild and Other Stories*. New York: Seven Stories, 1996. 3–29. Print.

———. *Dawn*. New York: Warner, 1987. Print.

———. *Kindred*. Boston: Beacon, 1979. Print.

———. "A Necessary Being." Butler, *Unexpected* n.p.

———. *Survivor*. Garden City: Doubleday, 1978.

———. *Unexpected Stories*. New York: Open Road, 2014. Kindle file.

———. *Wild Seed*. New York: Aspect-Warner, 1980. Print.

Byerman, Keith E. *Fingering the Jagged Grain: Tradition and Form in Recent Black Fiction*. Athens: U of Georgia P, 1985. Print.

———. *Remembering the Past in Contemporary African American Fiction*. Chapel Hill: U of North Carolina P, 2005. Print.

Calveri, John. "Janelle Monáe: A New Pioneer of Afrofuturism." *Black Sky Thinking*. The Quietus, 2 Sept. 2010. Web. 24 July 2014.

Canavan, Gerry. "Knowing No One's Listening." Rev. of *Unexpected Stories*, by Octavia E. Butler. *Los Angeles Review of Books* 6 June 2014. Web. 6 July 2015.

Cartwright, Keith. *Sacral Grooves, Limbo Gateways: Travels in Deep Southern Time, Circum-Caribbean Space, Afro-creole Authority*. Athens: U of Georgia P, 2013. Print. New Southern Stud.

"Chanting 'Black Lives Matter,' Protesters Shut Down Part of Mall of America." Associated Press. NYTimes.com. New York Times, 20 Dec. 2014. Web. 3 Jan. 2015.

Chodorow, Nancy. *The Reproduction of Mothering: Psychoanalysis and the Sociology of Gender*. 2nd ed. Berkeley: U of California P, 1978. Print.

Clemons, Walter. "The Ghosts of 'Sixty Million and More.'" *Newsweek* 28 Sept. 1987: 75.

Clockshop. *Radio Imagination: Artists and Writers in the Archive of Octavia E. Butler.* Los Angeles: Clockshop, 27 Jan. 2016. Web. 2 June 2016.

Cobb, Jelani. "The Matter of Black Lives: A New Kind of Movement Found Its Moment. What Will Its Future Be?" *The New Yorker.* The New Yorker, 14 March 2016. Web. 1 June 2016.

Collins, Patricia Hill. "The Meaning of Motherhood in Black Culture and Black Mother–Daughter Relationships." 1987. Bell-Scott et al. 42–60.

"Concerning Cindi and the Glow of the Drogon's Eyes." *The Electric Lady.* Tumblr. n.d. Web. 21 July 2014.

Dash, Julie. *Daughters of the Dust.* Screenplay. Dash, *Daughters of the Dust: The Making* 75–164 [1–90].

———. *Daughters of the Dust: The Making of an African American Woman's Film.* New York: New P, 1992. Print.

———. "Making *Daughters of the Dust.*" Dash, *Daughters of the Dust: The Making* 1–26.

Dash, Julie, and Houston A. Baker Jr. "Not without My Daughters." *Transition* 57 (1992): 150–66. Web. 28 Jan. 2011.

Daughters of the Dust. Dir. Julie Dash. Kino International, 1991. DVD.

David, Marlo. "Afrofuturism and Post-Soul Possibility in Black Popular Music." *African American Review* 41.4 (2007): 695–707. Web. 2 June 2010.

Davis, Mary Kemp. "Everybody Knows Her Name: The Recovery of the Past in Sherley Anne Williams's *Dessa Rose.*" *Callaloo* 40 (1989): 544–58. Web. 11 Dec. 2015.

Dayen, David. "Black America Is Getting Screwed: Shocking New Study Highlights the Depths of Economic Disparities." *Salon,* 2 June 2015. Web. 10 Aug. 2015.

Deleuze, Gilles, and Félix Guattari. *A Thousand Plateaus: Capitalism and Schizophrenia.* Trans. Brian Massumi. Minneapolis: U of Minnesota P, 1987. Print.

Demetrakopoulos, Stephanie A. "Maternal Bonds as Devourers of Women's Individuation in Toni Morrison's *Beloved.*" *African American Review* 26.1 (1992): 51–59. Web. 11 Dec. 2015.

Dery, Mark. "Black to the Future: Interviews with Samuel R. Delany, Greg Tate, and Tricia Rose." *Flame Wars: The Discourse of Cyberculture.* Ed. Mark Dery. Durham: Duke UP, 1994. 179–221. Print.

Dick, Philip K. *Do Androids Dream of Electric Sheep?* New York: Ballantine, 1968. Print.

Dubey, Madhu. "Gayl Jones and the Matrilineal Metaphor of Tradition." *Signs* 20.2 (1995): 245–67. Web. 2 June 2011.

Du Bois, W. E. B. *The Souls of Black Folk.* Boston: Bedford, 1997. Print. Bedford Ser. in History and Culture.

English, Daylanne K., and Alvin Kim. "Now We Want Our Funk Cut: Janelle Monáe's Neo-Afrofuturism." *American Studies* 52.4 (2013): 217–30. Web. 9 June 2016.

Eshun, Kodwo. "Further Considerations on Afrofuturism." *New Centennial Review* 3.2 (2003): 287–302. Web. 20 Nov. 2010.

———. *More Brilliant than the Sun: Adventures in Sonic Fiction.* London: Quartet, 1998. Print.

Fanon, Frantz. *Black Skin, White Masks.* London: Pluto, 1967. Web. 27 May 2015.

Flagel, Nadine. "'It's Almost Like Being There': Speculative Fiction, Slave Narrative, and the Crisis of Representation in Octavia Butler's Kindred." *Canadian Review of American Studies* 42.2 (2012): 216–45. Web. 6 July 2015.

Foster, Gwendolyn Audrey. "Julie Dash: 'I think we need to do more than try to document history.'" *Women Filmmakers of the African and Asian Diaspora: Decolonizing the Gaze, Locating Subjectivity*. Carbondale: Southern Illinois UP, 1997. 43–72. Print.

Francis, Conseula. *Conversations with Octavia Butler*. Jackson: UP of Mississippi, 2009. Print. Lit. Conversations Ser.

Franklin, Krista. *Do Androids Dream of How People Are Sheep?* 2010. Mixed media on watercolor paper. 24700. California Institute of the Arts, 10 Nov. 2014. Web. 12 Aug. 2015.

Franklin, Krista, and T. L. Andrews. "Futures // Afrofuturism: An Interview with Krista Franklin." *BerlinArtLink.com*. Berlin Art Link, 21 Jun. 2016. Web. 1 July 2016.

Franklin, Krista, and Tempestt Hazel. "Black to the Future Series: An Interview with Krista Franklin." *The Chicago Arts Archive*. Sixty Inches from Center, 28 May 2012. Web. 10 Aug. 2015.

Fuss, Diana. "Interior Colonies: Frantz Fanon and the Politics of Identification." *Diacritics* 24.2 (Summer 1994): 20–42. Web. 27 May 2015.

Gallop, Jane. *The Daughter's Seduction: Feminism and Psychoanalysis*. Ithaca: Cornell UP, 1982. Print.

Gilroy, Paul. *The Black Atlantic: Modernity and Double Consciousness*. Cambridge: Harvard UP, 1993. Print.

———. *Small Acts: Thoughts on the Politics of Black Cultures*. London: Serpent's Tail, 1993. Print.

Glissant, Édouard. *Caribbean Discourse: Selected Essays*. Charlottesville: UP of Virginia, 1989. Print. Caraf Books Ser.

Gonzales, Michael A. "[BLACK ALT] What Is Afrofuturism?" *Ebony*. Ebony, 1 Oct. 2013. Web. 24 July 2014.

Goyal, Yogita. "From Return to Redemption: Caryl Phillips and Postcolonial Hybridity." *Romance, Diaspora, and Black Atlantic Literature*. New York: Cambridge UP, 2010. Web. 20 Feb. 2015.

Grandt, Jürgen E. *Kinds of Blue: The Jazz Aesthetic in African American Narrative*. Columbus: Ohio State UP, 2004. Print

———. *Shaping Words to Fit the Soul: The Southern Ritual Grounds of Afro-Modernism*. Columbus: Ohio State UP, 2009. Print.

Gunn, James, and Karen Hellekson. Foreword. *Future Females, the Next Generation: New Voices and Velocities in Feminist Science Fiction Criticism*. Ed. Marleen S. Barr. Lanham: Rowman, 2000. ix–xi. Print.

Halberstam, Judith [J. Jack], and Ira Livingston, eds. "Posthuman Bodies." Introduction. *Posthuman Bodies*. Bloomington: Indiana UP, 1995. 1–19. Print.

Hall, Stuart. "On Postmodernism and Articulation: An Interview with Stuart Hall." Ed. Lawrence Grossberg. *Stuart Hall: Critical Dialogues in Cultural Studies*. Ed. David

Morley and Kuan-Hsing Chen. London: Routledge, 1996. 131–50. Web. 9 June 2016.

Haraway, Donna J. "A Cyborg Manifesto: Science, Technology, and Socialist-Feminism in the Late Twentieth Century." *Simians, Cyborgs, and Women: The Reinvention of Nature*. New York: Routledge, 1991. 149–81. Print.

Harb, Sirène. "Memory, History and Self-Reconstruction in Gayl Jones's *Corregidora*." *Journal of Modern Literature* 31.3 (2008): 116–36. Web. 14 June 2011.

Hayles, N. Katherine. *How We Became Posthuman: Virtual Bodies in Cybernetics, Literature, and Informatics*. Chicago: U of Chicago P, 1999. Print.

Hirsch, Marianne. *The Mother/Daughter Plot: Narrative Psychoanalysis, Feminism*. Bloomington: Indiana UP, 1989. Print.

hooks, bell. "Postmodern Blackness." *Yearning: Race, Gender, and Cultural Politics*. Boston: South End, 1990. 23–31. Print.

Horwitz, Deborah. "Nameless Ghosts: Possession and Dispossession in *Beloved*." *Studies in American Fiction* 17.2 (1989): 157–67. Web. 7 July 2015.

Imarisha, Walidah, and adrienne maree brown, ed. *Octavia's Brood: Science Fiction Stories from Social Justice Movements*. Oakland: AK Press, 2015. Print.

Iton, Richard. *In Search of the Black Fantastic*. Oxford: Oxford UP, 2008. Print.

Jackson, Zakiyyah Iman. "Animal: New Directions in the Theorization of Race and Posthumanism." *Feminist Studies* 39.3 (2013): 669–85. Web. 30 Jan. 2015.

Jamieson, Dave, Emran Hossain, and Kim Bhasin. "How Bangladesh Garment Industry Traded Workplace Safety for Jobs." *Huff Post Business*. The Huffington Post, 23 May 2013. Web. 10 Aug. 2015.

Johnson, E. Patrick. *Appropriating Blackness: Performance and the Politics of Authenticity*. Durham: Duke UP, 2003. Print.

Jones, Gayl. *Corregidora*. New York: Random, 1975. Print.

———. *Liberating Voices: Oral Tradition in African American Literature*. Cambridge, MA: Harvard UP, 1991. Print.

Jones, Gayl, and Michael S. Harper. "Gayl Jones: An Interview." *Massachusetts Review* 18.4 (1977): 692–715. Web. 17 June 2011.

Jones, Peter Carr. "Blue Notes." *Encyclopedia of African American History*. Ed. Leslie M. Alexander and Walter C. Rucker. Vol. 1. Santa Barbara: ABC-Clio, 2010. 165–66. Print.

Joseph, Gloria I. "Black Mothers and Daughters: Traditional and New Perspectives." Bell-Scott et al. 94–106.

Karavanta, Mina. "Toni Morrison's *A Mercy* and the Counterwriting of Negative Communities: A Postnational Novel." *Modern Fiction Studies* 58.4 (Winter 2012): 723–46. Web. 7 July 2015.

Kirkus Reviews. Rev. of *Unexpected Stories*, by Octavia E. Butler. *Kirkus* 24 June 2014. Web. 6 July 2015.

Kristeva, Julia. "Approaching Abjection." *Powers of Horror: An Essay on Abjection*. New York: Columbia UP, 1982. 1–31. Print.

Kubitschek, Missy Dehn. *Claiming the Heritage: African-American Women Novelists and History.* Jackson: UP of Mississippi, 1991. Print.

Lacan, Jacques. *Écrits.* Trans. Alan Sheridan. New York: Norton, 1977. Print.

Lacey, Lauren J. *The Past That Might Have Been, the Future That May Come: Women Writing Fantastic Fiction, 1960s to the Present.* Jefferson, NC: McFarland, 2014. Print. Critical Explorations in Science Fiction and Fantasy.

Lecrivain, Marie, ed. *Near Kin: A Collection of Words and Art Inspired by Octavia Estelle Butler.* Los Angeles: Sybaritic, 2014. Print.

Lillvis, Kristen. "Mama's Baby, Papa's Slavery? The Problems and Promise of Mothering in Octavia E. Butler's 'Bloodchild.'" MELUS 39.4 (Winter 2014): 7–22. Print.

Loichot, Valérie. "'We are all related': Edouard Glissant Meets Octavia Butler." *Small Axe* 30 (2009): 37–50. Web. 20 Feb. 2015.

Long, Lisa. "A Relative Pain: The Rape of History in Octavia Butler's *Kindred* and Phyllis Alesia Perry's *Stigmata.*" *College English* 64.4 (March 2002): 459–83. Web. 25 June 2015.

Lorde, Audre. *Sister Outsider.* Berkeley: Crossing P, 1984. Print. Crossing P Feminist Ser.

Lowinsky, Naomi Ruth. *Stories from the Motherline: Reclaiming the Mother-Daughter Bond, Finding Our Feminine Souls.* Los Angeles: Tarcher, 1992. Print.

Macpherson, C. B. *The Political Theory of Possessive Individuation: Hobbes to Locke.* Oxford: Oxford UP, 1962. Print.

Mason, Carol. "Terminating Bodies: Toward a Cyborg History of Abortion." *Posthuman Bodies.* Ed. Judith Halberstam and Ira Livingston. Bloomington: Indiana UP, 1995. *Net Library.* Web. 10 Apr. 2010. 225–43.

Mayer, Ruth. "'Africa as an Alien Future': The Middle Passage, Afrofuturism, and Postcolonial Waterworlds." *Amerikastudien* 45.4 (2000): 554–66. Print.

Melzer, Patricia. *Alien Constructions: Science Fiction and Feminist Thought.* Austin: U of Texas P, 2006. Print.

Misrahi-Barak, Judith. "Post-*Beloved* Writing: Review, Revitalize, Recalculate." *Black Studies Papers* 1.1 (2014): 37–55. Web. 19 Aug. 2015.

Monáe, Janelle. "Q.U.E.E.N." Feat. Erykah Badu. *The Electric Lady.* Wondaland Arts Society and Bad Boy Records, 2013. Music Video. Dir. Alan Ferguson. *YouTube.* 21 July 2014.

Montgomery, Maxine L. "Got on My Traveling Shoes: Migration, Exile, and Home in Toni Morrison's *A Mercy.*" *Journal of Black Studies* 42.4 (2011): 627–37. Web. 7 July 2015.

Moody, Joycelyn K. "Ripping Away the Veil of Slavery: Literacy, Communal Love, and Self-Esteem in Three Slave Women's Narratives." *Black American Literature Forum* 24.4 (Winter 1990): 633–48. Web. 11 Dec. 2015.

Moore, Geneva Cobb. "A Demonic Parody: Toni Morrison's *A Mercy.*" *Southern Literary Journal* 44.1 (Fall 2011): 1–19. Web. 7 July 2015.

Moraga, Cherríe. Preface. *This Bridge Called My Back: Writings by Radical Women of*

Color. Ed. Cherríe Moraga and Gloria Anzaldúa. Watertown, Mass.: Persephone, 1981. xiii–xix. Print.

Morgenstern, Naomi. "Maternal Love/Maternal Violence: Inventing Ethics in Toni Morrison's *A Mercy*." MELUS 39.1 (Spring 2014): 7–29. Web. 7 July 2015.

Morrison, Toni. *Beloved*. New York: Plume-Penguin, 1987. Print.

———. "Home." *The House That Race Built: Original Essays by Toni Morrison, Angela Y. Davis, Cornel West, and Others on Black Americans and Politics in America Today*. Ed. Wahneema Lubiano. New York: Vintage-Random, 1998. 3–12. Print.

———. Interview by Stephen Colbert. *The Colbert Report*. Comedy Central, 19 Nov. 2014. Web. 20 Nov. 2014.

———. *A Mercy*. New York: Vintage-Random, 2008. Print.

Murray, Albert. *Stomping the Blues*. New York: McGraw-Hill, 1976. Print.

O'Brien, John. "Syracuse University Students March in Protest of Missouri Grand Jury Decision in Death of Michael Brown." *Syracuse.com*. The Post-Standard, 1 Dec. 2014. Web. 31 Dec. 2014.

O'Reilly, Andrea. *Toni Morrison and Motherhood: A Politics of the Heart*. Albany: State U of New York P, 2004. Print.

Parham, Marisa. "Saying 'Yes': Textual Traumas in Octavia Butler's *Kindred*." *Callaloo* 32.4 (Fall 2009): 1315–31. Web. 9 June 2015.

Passalacqua, Camille. "Witnessing to Heal the Self in Gayl Jones's *Corregidora* and Phyllis Alesia Perry's *Stigmata*." MELUS 35.4 (2010): 139–63. Web. 14 June 2011.

Passariello, Christina, and Suzanne Kapner. "Search for Ever Cheaper Garment Factories Leads to Africa." *Wall Street Journal*, 12 July 2015. Web. 10 Aug. 2015.

Patton, Venetria K. *Women in Chains: The Legacy of Slavery in Black Women's Fiction*. Albany: State U of New York P, 2000. Print. SUNY Ser. in Afro-Amer. Studies.

Pelton, Robert D. *The Trickster in West Africa: A Study of Mythic Irony and Sacred Delight*. Berkeley: U of California P, 1980. Print. Hermeneutics: Studies in the Hist. of Religions.

Phillips, John. "Agencement/Assemblage." *Theory, Culture, and Society* 23.2–3 (2006): 108–09. Web. 1 June 2016.

Primeau, Jamie. "All of Beyoncé's *Lemonade* References and Cameos in One Handy Chart." *Bustle*. Bustle, 28 April 2016. Web. 6 July 2016.

Puar, Jasbir K. "'I would rather be a cyborg than a goddess': Becoming-Intersectional in Assemblage Theory." *philoSOPHIA* 2.1 (2012): 49–66. Web. 27 May 2016.

Randhawa, Kiran. "Thousands Protest outside U.S. Embassy in London over Michael Brown Shooting." *London Evening Standard Online*. London Evening Standard, 27 Nov. 2014. Web. 3 Jan. 2015.

Raynaud, Claudine. "The Poetics of Abjection in *Beloved*." *Black Imagination and the Middle Passage*. Ed. Maria Diedrich, Henry Louis Gates Jr., and Carl Pedersen. W. E. B. Du Bois Inst. New York: Oxford UP, 1999. 70–85. Print.

Roberts, Kamaria, and Kenya Downs. "What Beyoncé Teaches Us about the African Diaspora in *Lemonade*." Art Beat. PBS *NewsHour*, 29 April 2016. Web. 7 July 2016.

Rody, Caroline. *The Daughter's Return: African-American and Caribbean Women's Fictions of History*. New York: Oxford UP, 2001. Print.

Roye, Susmita. "Toni Morrison's Disrupted Girls and Their Disturbed Girlhoods: *The Bluest Eye* and *A Mercy*." *Callaloo* 35.1 (Winter 2012): 212–27. Web. 7 July 2015.

Rule, Sheila. "Director Defies Odds with First Feature, *Daughters of the Dust*." *New York Times* 12 Feb. 1992: C15+. ProQuest. Web. 28 Jan. 2011.

Rushdy, Ashraf H. A. *Neo–Slave Narratives: Studies in the Social Logic of a Literary Form*. Oxford: Oxford UP, 1999. Print.

———. "Reading Mammy: The Subject of Relation in Sherley Anne Williams' *Dessa Rose*." *African American Review* 27.3 (Autumn 1993): 365–89. Web. 11 Dec. 2015.

———. *Remembering Generations: Race and Family in Contemporary African American Fiction*. Chapel Hill: U of North Carolina P, 2001. Print.

Ryan, Tim A. *Calls and Responses: The American Novel of Slavery Since Gone with the Wind*. Baton Rouge: Louisiana State UP, 2008. Print.

Sandoval, Chela. *The Methodology of the Oppressed*. Minneapolis: U of Minnesota P, 2000. Print.

Schapiro, Barbara. "The Bonds of Love and the Boundaries of the Self in Toni Morrison's *Beloved*." *Contemporary Literature* 32.2 (1991): 194–210. Web. 7 July 2015.

Schueller, Malini Johar. "Analogy and (White) Feminist Theory: Thinking Race and the Color of the Cyborg Body." *Signs* 31.1 (2005): 63–92. Web. 11 May 2010.

Schuessler, Jennifer. "Dialect Society Names Its Word of the Year: #blacklivesmatter." *NYTimes.com*. New York Times, 10 Jan. 2015. Web. 11 Jan. 2015.

Sharkey, Greg. "Ferguson Missouri: Bloody Sunday Families Show Solidarity with Victim." *Derry Journal*. Derry Journal, 1 Dec. 2014. Web. 31 Dec. 2014.

Smith, Valerie. "Neo–Slave Narratives." *The Cambridge Companion to the African American Slave Narrative*. Ed. Audrey Fisch. New York: Cambridge UP, 2007. 168–85. Print.

Spillers, Hortense J. "Mama's Baby, Papa's Maybe: An American Grammar Book." *Diacritics* 17.2 (1987): 64–81. JSTOR. Web. 3 Apr. 2012.

Spratt, Sam. Album cover. *The Electric Lady*. By Janelle Monáe, Wondaland Arts Society and Bad Boy Records, 2013.

———. Album cover. *The Electric Lady: Deluxe Edition*. By Janelle Monáe, Wondaland Arts Society and Bad Boy Records, 2013.

Steinberg, Marc. "Inverting History in Octavia Butler's Postmodern Slave Narrative." *African American Review* 38.3 (2004): 467–76. Web. 25 June 2015.

Tal, Kalí. "The Unbearable Whiteness of Being: African American Critical Theory and Cyberculture." *KaliTal.com*. n.d. Web. 21 Oct. 2010.

Tate, Greg, and Arthur Jafa. "La Vénus Nègre." *Artforum* 30.5 (1992): 90–93. Web. 28 Jan. 2011.

Taylor, Matthew A. *Universes without Us: Posthuman Cosmologies in American Literature*. Minneapolis: U of Minnesota P, 2013. Print.

Thaler, Ingrid. *Black Atlantic Speculative Fictions: Octavia E. Butler, Jewelle Gomez, and Nalo Hopkinson*. New York: Routledge, 2010. Print. Research in Atlantic Stud. 2.

Thomas, Sheree Renée. "How Sukie Cross de Big Wata." *Mojo: Conjure Stories*. Ed. Nalo Hopkinson. New York: Aspect-Warner, 2003. 326–34. Print.

Thompson, Carlyle Van. "Miscegenation, Monstrous Memories, and Misogyny as Sexual Consumption in Gayl Jones' *Corregidora*." *Eating the Black Body: Miscegenation as Sexual Consumption in African American Literature and Culture*. New York: Peter Lang, 2006. 71–106. Print.

Trapasso, Ann E. "Returning to the Site of Violence: The Restructuring of Slavery's Legacy in Sherley Anne Williams's *Dessa Rose*." *Violence, Silence, and Anger: Women's Writing as Transgression*. Ed. Deirdre Lashgari. Charlottesville: U of Virginia P, 1995. 219–30. Print. Feminist Issues: Practice, Politics, Theory.

Wallace, Michele. *Invisibility Blues: From Pop to Theory*. London: Verso, 1990. Print.

Warren, Calvin L. "Black Nihilism and the Politics of Hope." *CR: The New Centennial Review* 15.1 (Spring 2015): 215–48. Web. 31 May 2015.

Washuta, Elissa. "The Wrongheaded Obsession with 'Vanishing' Indigenous Peoples." *Salon*. 24 Nov. 2013. Web. 23 July 2014.

Weheliye, Alexander G. "'Feenin': Posthuman Voices in Contemporary Black Popular Music." *Social Text* 20.2 (2002): 21–47. Web. 2 June 2010.

———. *Habeas Viscus: Racializing Assemblages, Biopolitics, and Black Feminist Theories of the Human*. Durham: Duke UP, 2014. Print.

Wilkerson, Abby. "Ending at the Skin: Sexuality and Race in Feminist Thinking." *Hypatia* 12.3 (1997): 164–73. Web. 11 May 2010.

Williams, Sherley Anne. Author's Note. Williams 5–6.

———. *Dessa Rose*. New York: HarperCollins, 1986. Print.

Willis, Roy. "Eshu the Trickster." *World Mythology*. New York: Holt, 1993. 274–75. Print.

Winchell, Donna Haisty. "Cries of Outrage: Three Novelists' Use of History." *Mississippi Quarterly* 9.4 (Fall 1996): 727–41. Web. 11 Dec. 2015.

Womack, Ytasha L. *Afrofuturism: The World of Black Sci-Fi and Fantasy Culture*. Chicago: Lawrence Hill Books–Chicago Review P, 2013. Print.

Wondaland Arts Society. About. *Wondaland Arts Society*. 2014. Web. 23 July 2014.

Woolfork, Lisa. *Embodying American Slavery in Contemporary Culture*. Champaign: U of Illinois P, 2008. Print.

Wyatt, Jean. "Failed Messages, Maternal Loss, and Narrative Form in Toni Morrison's *A Mercy*." *Modern Fiction Studies* 58.1 (Spring 2012): 128–51. Web. 7 July 2015.

———. "Giving Body to the Word: The Maternal Symbolic in Toni Morrison's *Beloved*." *PMLA* 108.3 (1993): 474–88. Web. 7 July 2015.

Wynter, Sylvia. "Beyond the Word of Man: Glissant and the New Discourse of the Antilles." *World Literature Today* 63.4 (Autumn 1989): 637–48. Web. 20 Feb. 2015.

———. "On Disenchanting Discourse: 'Minority' Literary Criticism and Beyond." *Cultural Critique* 7 (1987): 207–44. Web. 7 March 2015.

Yaszek, Lisa. "Afrofuturism, Science Fiction, and the History of the Future." *Socialism and Democracy Online* 20.3 (2006): 41–60. Web. 11 May 2014.

———. "An Afrofuturist Reading of Ralph Ellison's *Invisible Man*." *Rethinking History: The Journal of Theory and Practice* 9.2–3 (2005): 297–313. Web. 11 May 2014.

———. "'A Grim Fantasy': Remaking American History in Octavia Butler's *Kindred*." *Signs* 28.4 (2003): 1053–66. Web. 17 June 2015.

———. *The Self Wired: Technology and Subjectivity in Contemporary Narrative*. New York: Routledge, 2002. Print.

Zoladz, Lindsay. "Take Cover: Janelle Monáe's *The Electric Lady*." *Pitchfork*. Pitchfork Media, 9 Sept. 2013. Web. 7 July 2016.

abject, 105, 111–12

Afrofuturism, 119n3 (intro); aesthetic, 2, 3, 58, 63; in art, 2–3, 7, 59; definitions of, 2–3, 7, 58–60, 63, 68, 69, 81, 86; film, 6–7, 10; important figures in, 58, 64, 79; and liminality, 2–3, 7, 58–62, 64, 68, 78, 83, 97, 100; in literature, 3, 7, 9, 58, 69, 78, 83, 86; in music, 3, 7, 9, 58–60, 64, 65, 69, 76, 78; in music videos, 6–7, 9, 10, 59, 64, 65–69. *See also* Badu, Erykah; Butler, Octavia E.; Eshun, Kodwo; Monáe, Janelle

agency, 24, 55, 80, 111, 112; and posthuman liminality, 4, 9, 13, 27, 70, 117

alienation, 2, 81, 83, 86, 120n1 (chap. 4)

aliens: abduction by, 83, 86; characteristics of, 4, 93–94, 97; environment of, 82, 93–94, 107

antebellum South: architecture of, 6; history of, 43, 56, 57; as setting, 8, 39, 48, 51, 86, 87, 89

Appiah, Kwame Anthony, 4–5

assemblage, 10, 14, 40, 42, 45, 51–55

authenticity. *See* blackness: authentic; essentialism

Badu, Erykah, 9, 63; in Afrofuturism, 58, 64; and Afrofuturist liminality, 58–59, 64–66, 78; and humanism, black, 64, 65; as Oblongata, Badoula, 66; and time travel, 64

—works: "Gone Baby, Don't Be Long,"

64–66; "Next Lifetime," 64–66; "On & On," 64; "Window Seat," 59

Baker, Houston A., 72–73

Basu, Biman, 54, 56

Baucom, Ian, 101–03, 111

Beaulieu, Elizabeth Ann, 6, 13, 120n2 (chap. 1)

becoming-subject, 3, 9, 13, 21–22, 24, 27, 29, 31, 34; definitions of, 14–15, 40–41, 44–45. *See also* Halberstam, Judith [J. Jack]; Livingston, Ira; Morrison, Toni; Williams, Sherley Anne

Beloved (Morrison), 36, 73, 116, 119n1 (chap. 1), 120nn2–3 (chap. 1); as neo-slave narrative, 8, 98; and posthuman community, 45, 78; and posthuman liminality, 8, 11, 12, 13, 13–27, 28, 29; as speculative fiction, 97

Benjamin, Jessica, 21

Beyoncé, 10; *Lemonade*, 6–7, 10

birth: of children, 9, 20, 43, 49, 76, 104–06, 108, 112, 116; rebirth, 6, 20, 24, 79, 109; of self, 105; of stories 72, 73

Black Atlantic, 2, 60, 86

black feminism, 6, 113

#blacklivesmatter (Black Lives Matter), 38–39, 119n2 (intro), 120nn1–2 (chap. 2)

blackness, 8, 83; authentic, 61–62, 63, 65–67, 69; postmodern, 2; semiotics of, 81–85, 91; and whiteness, 9, 46, 61, 81, 82–85, 87, 88–89, 91–93. *See also* posthuman blackness

O'Reilly, Andrea, 13, 14, 18, 21, 22, 120n2 (chap. 1)

patriarchy, 40, 43, 52, 54, 57
police brutality, 38, 120nn1–2 (chap. 2)
postcolonialism, 5, 6, 63, 100, 114
posthuman blackness: and Afrofuturism, 58, 59, 65, 81, 92; definitions of, 2, 4, 9, 71, 92, 99; and Glissant, 100, 103; and liminality, 59, 65, 66, 81, 99, 100, 117
posthumanism: and community, 9, 26–27, 39, 41–42, 43–48, 54, 57, 69, 76–78; and liminality, 3–4, 6–10, 11, 12, 21, 24, 40–41, 44–45, 58–59, 85, 92, 99, 101–03, 107, 117; and solidarity, 9, 39–40, 41–54, 56–57, 81, 116. *See also* Butler, Octavia E.; Dash, Julie; Jones, Gayl; Monáe, Janelle; Morrison, Toni; multiple consciousness, posthuman; Thomas, Sheree Renée; Williams, Sherley Anne
postmodernism, 2, 4, 5, 6, 63
poststructuralism, 4, 5, 6, 63
psychoanalysis: 20–22, 82, 107–08; and psychosexual development, 15, 19–20, 99, 104–06, 110, 120n3 (chap.1), 121n3 (chap. 5). *See also* becoming-subject; language; relational triangle
Puar, Jasbir K., 4, 40, 119n1 (intro)

"Q.U.E.E.N." (Monáe), 58–59, 66–69

racialization, 41, 47, 53
racism, 41, 48, 56, 88, 94, 102, 116
rebirth, 6, 20, 24, 79, 109
relational triangle, 17–18, 20–22, 27–31, 33–34, 35–37, 120n3 (chap. 1). *See also* Chodorow, Nancy; Morrison, Toni
Rody, Caroline, 6, 13, 23, 26, 63, 113, 116
Rule, Sheila, 111, 117

Rushdy, Ashraf H. A., 8, 48–49, 51, 75–76, 78, 120n3 (chap. 2)

science fiction, 1, 7–9, 69, 79, 81, 83, 86, 94, 97, 119n3 (intro). *See also* speculative fiction
semiotics, 81–85, 91
slavery: and cultural identity, 8, 62, 94, 100–02; and family, 15, 18–19, 21, 29, 33–34; freedom from, 50, 81, 108-10; 112; and individual identity, 8, 27, 35, 55–56, 89, 109–10, 120n4 (chap. 1), 120n3 (chap. 3); and modernity, 2, 80, 82, 120n4 (chap. 4); and trauma, 11, 13, 31, 72, 82. *See also* Butler, Octavia E.; Dash, Julie; Glissant, Édouard; Jones, Gayl; Middle Passage; Monáe, Janelle; Morrison, Toni; neo–slave narratives; Thomas, Sheree Renée; Williams, Sherley Anne
solidarity, posthuman, 9, 39–40, 41–54, 56–57, 81, 116
speculative fiction, 9, 42, 78, 81, 97, 98–99, 119n3 (intro). *See also* science fiction
Spillers, Hortense, 5, 71, 120n3 (chap. 3), 121n3 (chap. 5), 121n5 (chap. 5)
Spratt, Sam, 58, 120n1 (chap. 3)
Star Trek, 3, 59
Steinberg, Marc, 87–88, 91
submarine (Glissant), 99, 100–11, 115, 116; in works by Dash, Julie, 110, 115–16; in works by Thomas, Sheree Renée, 104, 106, 108–10
Sun Ra, 58
Superdome, 6, 119n2

Tal, Kalí, 7, 12, 64, 100, 119n1 (intro)
Thomas, Sheree Renée: "How Sukie Cross de Big Wata," 9, 98, 99, 104–10; and language, nonrepresentational, 98, 106–07, 108–09, 110–11; and post-

Printed in the United States
By Bookmasters